Rachel Smiles

Other Books by Darrell Scott

Rachel's Tears
(with Beth Nimmo and Steve Rabey)

Chain Reaction
(with Steve Rabey)

Rachel Smiles

The Spiritual Legacy of Columbine Martyr Rachel Scott

Darrell Scott

Steve Rabey

THOMAS NELSON PUBLISHERS®
Nashville

A Division of Thomas Nelson, Inc.
www.ThomasNelson.com

Published in Nashville, Tennessee, by Thomas Nelson, Inc.

Unless otherwise noted, Scripture references are from the HOLY BIBLE: NEW INTERNA-
TIONAL VERSION®. Copyright © 1973, 1978, 1984 by International Bible Society. Used by
permission of Zondervan Publishing House. All rights reserved.

Scripture quotations noted NASB are from the NEW AMERICAN STANDARD BIBLE', ©
Copyright The Lockman Foundation 1960, 1962, 1963, 1968, 1971, 1972, 1973, 1975, 1977
Used by permission. (www.lockman.org)

Scripture quotations noted NKJV are from THE NEW KING JAMES VERSION. Copyright © 1979,
1980, 1982, Thomas Nelson, Inc. Publishers.

Scripture quotations noted KJV are from the KING JAMES VERSION.

ISBN: 978-0-7852-9688-1

Printed in the United States of America

02 03 04 05 06 PHX 5 4 3 2 1

Dedication

This book is dedicated to my youngest son, Michael David Scott. Mike, you grieved deeply but quietly for the loss of your sister. My heart broke for you many times as I watched your pain. I know how much you loved Rachel, and I pray that your life will be as yielded to Jesus as hers was.

Rachel with her brother Mike

It was three in the morning when I woke up to see you drawing the following picture. You were fourteen years old and had just joined me on a speaking engagement in Georgia, but you were still awake, and I watched as you slowly drew this tribute to Rachel. I saw the tears in your eyes as you drew the tears in her eyes. I also sensed the pain you were feeling. I know how close you and Rachel were, and I want you to know she would be proud of you. You are one of the reasons she smiles!

Picture Mike drew of Rachel's tears

I love you, Mike.

Dad

Contents

Acknowledgments

There are so many people I want to thank for helping contribute to this publication. I am sure that I will overlook someone, but if I do, please forgive me and know that you are appreciated.

My wife, Sandy, has been an incredible support in this endeavor. Sandy, I love you and thank you.

Thanks to Paul Jackson, Barry and Sue Kraft, Danny Orr, Bill Sanders, and Scott Dodge, who comprise our Columbine Redemption staff and speakers.

Thanks to Carrie Liebich for her volunteer help.

Thanks to Dana Scott for the many hours on the road speaking to thousands of young people and parents. Thanks to my other children: Bethanee and Don McCandless, Ryan, Belinda, and Noah (our first grandchild!), Cory, Tyler, Craig, and Mike. Your love and support are priceless.

Special thanks to Steve Rabey for helping complete this book.

Thanks to the many friends around the world who have prayed for us faithfully. I will write only a partial list of close friends who have been there with us and for us: Wayne and Betsy Worthy, Bob and Judith Mumford and family, Josh and Dottie McDowell, David Barton, John Craig, Jeff Deyo, DeVerne Fromke, Bob and Terry Cornuke, Foster and Lynn Friess, Tom Lang, Pastor J.R. and the Church of the Rock, Dave and Chris Sprenger, Steve Rabey, Frank Amedia and family, Bryan and Nancy Boorujy, Adam Brandley, John and Doreen Tomlin, Grandma Kaye, Danny and Sarah

Scott, Wes Cantrell, David Briggs, Kelly Hadlich, Michael and Keren Kilgore, Mike Adamson and all the Campus Crusade staff, John Richmond and all the Youth for Christ network, Edgar and Yvonne Miles, Gary and Billie Jean Bauer, Jim and Renee May, John and Kimberly Curtis, Wes Yoder, Karen, Naomi, Charles, and all the Ambassador staff, all the folks from Thomas Nelson Publishing, Elizabeth Ridenour, Shane Hammond, Don Gordon, and a multitude of others who have been there for us.

Finally, special thanks to our prayer support team around the world, and those wonderful people who e-mailed us by the hundreds of thousands, and who are represented by a handful of those e-mails in this book.

Thank you all! You are the reason *Rachel Smiles*.

Special Appreciation

There are two special people that I want to express my deepest appreciation to. My wife, Sandy, and the administrator for the Columbine Redemption, Paul Jackson.

Sandy, words cannot begin to express my love for you as my wife and partner. You, more than anyone, have shown a commitment to a direction that we would have never chosen. I have watched you travel with me on an exhausting schedule, but I have never heard you complain. I have been encouraged by you at my lowest moments. I have seen your dedication to behind-the-scenes details without expectation of any acknowledgment. I have felt your support and love. Thank you. Because of you, Rachel smiles.

Paul Jackson, without your expertise and follow-up, we could never have reached the multitude of lives we have seen changed. You have proven to be a dedicated administrator with a passion for getting out our message to the masses. Your many hours of script writing and editing, your coordination of events and meetings, your phone calls, your sacrifices in traveling all have contributed to the smiles of Rachel. I love you as a friend and thank you as a coworker.

Foreword

All heroes are unusual. Most of us who accomplish anything amazing do so in the most indirect and unexpected manner. God's choice of persons whom He decides to use in some dramatic way is always a surprise. This was true in the Bible, and it is equally true in ordinary life. When trying to understand the surprising and the unexpected, we have coined the phrase "the scandal of the particular" to explain thoughts like "I know God can do the unusual, but not through her." We are almost offended when God chooses a particular person through whom He decides to reveal Himself. This whole idea can be illustrated in the life of Mary, the mother of our Lord Jesus Christ. She, most of all, was totally surprised that the almighty God had somehow chosen her. How could that possibly be? Think of the reactions of Joseph and her neighbors.

Allow me to say this so clearly that none of us could possibly miss it: "We have this treasure (God's glory) in earthen vessels." Jokingly, yet with more force than was originally intended, I like to rephrase the statement as, "We have this treasure in a Styrofoam cup."

Each of us who knew Rachel Scott in high school—her parents, her brothers and sisters, her high school friends, and others who surrounded her—knew she was a Styrofoam cup. Rachel was very human, unusually fragile, and frighteningly honest with herself and with others. Capable of thinking through the deeper issues, she was a living example of what it means to have this treasure in an earthen vessel.

This new book, *Rachel Smiles*, is an opportunity for you and me to see more clearly into the treasure that is God's glory. We refuse all attempts that would direct us toward some mistaken or utilitarian emphasis on the container. God's love and His own nature have chosen to continue to be revealed through this young lady. He has chosen to do so by means of her vital testimony, her writings, her unexpected death, and her daring spirit— revealed in the directness and openness of this serious and God-captivated teenager. Those of us who knew and loved her have discovered, or uncovered, more of this daily. You will discover some of it in her journals and the premonition of her life being given for Christ and His kingdom.

Darrell with Bob Mumford

As an insider, perhaps my role has been comparable to that of a spiritual uncle, because I have been involved with the Scott family for some twenty-five years. Immediately after the Columbine incident, Darrell and I talked through the pain. Together we sought to make sense of what appeared at the time to be a senseless tragedy without meaning or purpose. Without human effort—but not without grief, doubt, and much confusion—God's unfolding purpose began to emerge. Purpose, something more than we could understand, seemed to almost force itself upon the whole Scott family. It did so to the surprise and relief of her parents, her siblings, and all of us who were seeking to make this journey together.

Recently, the author, who is Rachel's father, came to our city to speak to the University of North Carolina's student body. The gymnasium quietly and rapidly filled to more than half—perhaps 1,200 students or so. They seemed thoughtful, pensive, and very expectant. Darrell stood to address them. The weight of what he had to say was evident on his face and in his voice. At no point in the ninety-minute talk did this gentle man depart from his assigned role of being there as Rachel's father. He carefully and intentionally refused the temptation of taking on some role of his own. Faithfully he presented the facts explaining the implications of Rachel's death. He courageously opened his own pain and that of her mother and of Rachel's brothers and sisters. This was her story. She was God's chosen instrument. The subject of this gathering was the glory that Rachel knew and wanted so badly to share with other students at Columbine and with young people around the world, such as those who poured into that gymnasium. The students unashamedly released welcome tears, commitment, openness, and response to Rachel's story.

Rachel's parents, her siblings, and this book, *Rachel Smiles,* seek to preserve that same purity of intent. The integrity that was exhibited here at UNC has been carefully preserved in the first two books, *Rachel's Tears* and *Chain Reaction.* I am thrilled to be able to say that this new book has managed to encapsulate and release this same integrity and purity. It is an honest attempt to explain more clearly and present more effectively the God and Father that Rachel Scott knew and sought to declare to others who needed Him.

God's own glory is the treasure. Would you consider allowing this young lady to take you by the hand and walk you into God's presence? Would you allow her to introduce you to the Lord Jesus whom she loved so deeply? Would you open yourself to the same risks that she did—of life and your future—for the purpose of making Him known to others who walk in darkness?

Rachel Smiles will encourage you to believe that the Lord Jesus Christ will eagerly deposit His treasure in you, with all your weakness and personal struggles, as He did in Rachel. You, too, can say with Rachel Scott, "These hands will touch hearts!"

The Bible says that God is eager to do more than we can ask or think. Certainly this promise has been fulfilled in the life of this ordinary young lady in whose earthen vessel God's glory humbly chose to reveal itself.

Bob Mumford
Author of *The Purpose of Temptation*

Introduction

The Story Continues

The book you are reading is the third phase of an amazing story that began on April 20, 1999.

On that day, two troubled young men armed with enough guns and bombs to start a small revolution opened fire at Columbine High School near Denver, Colorado, killing one teacher and twelve students and making the name Columbine an international symbol of tragedy.

One of the students killed that day was my daughter Rachel Joy Scott, who was outside the school having lunch with a friend.

My son Craig was more fortunate, but his youthful innocence was ripped from him that day. As he watched in horror, two of his best friends who huddled with him under a library table were murdered. Craig was able to tell his family about what happened to him that day, but information about the circumstances of Rachel's death was slower in coming. Even now, after a series of investigations and reports, there are still things we will never know about what happened that day.

Rachel's passing from this earth subjected me to a level of loss and grief I had never before known was possible. But as you will see in the pages that follow, this whole experience has changed my life in many other ways as well.

In the process of remembering Rachel's life and telling her story to others, I have found a renewed sense of purpose in life, experienced a sense of profound joy, and come to an entirely new appreciation of God's overwhelming love and grace.

A Journey of Discovery

Shortly after Rachel's death, we found a series of private journals she had kept. Reading these journals was like a revelation to us. In its pages we found her words, her drawings, her poems, her songs, and the many prayers she had written to God.

In addition, the journals also revealed a spiritual depth I had seen glimpses of over the years but had never seen before in such colorful detail. Even more astonishing, the journals showed that Rachel had experienced premonitions about her own death.

In a chilling entry written May 2, 1998, Rachel wrote:

> May 2nd
> This will be my last year Lord
> have gotten what can
> Thank you.

Another undated entry expressed similar sentiments:

Just passing by
Just coming thru
Not staying long
I always knew
This home I have
Will ~~never~~ never last

These and other revelations were the basis of *Rachel's Tears*, the first book written about Rachel, Columbine, and the significant impact this event would have in people's lives and hearts.

The second book, *Chain Reaction*, explored Rachel's philosophy of life and her unique approach to Christian service that formed the basis of her years at Columbine, her involvement at her church, and her relationships with her many friends. For example, she once expressed: "I have this theory that if one person can go out of their way to show compassion, then it will start a chain reaction of the same. People will never know how far a little kindness can go." *Chain Reaction* also discussed some of the many acts of compassion and selfless love she exhibited to so many people, including complete strangers, during her brief life.

Over the past two years, I have traveled the world speaking to groups about Rachel's philosophy and giving interviews to newspapers and television shows. I have been privileged to talk about Rachel with TV hosts like Oprah Winfrey and Katie Couric, and I have had the opportunity to share her story in schools, churches, community centers, arenas, and at outdoor festivals.

In every circumstance, I have encouraged those who heard me to put Rachel's philosophy into action, starting a "chain reaction" of their own and reaching out to others in a caring and Christlike manner. The warm response I have received has been both surprising and deeply gratifying.

Now, after three years of Rachel's story being told to millions of people, I feel that it's time for the next phase of the story.

A Lasting Legacy

Over the past three years, we have received an incredible number of letters, e-mails, and phone calls telling us about the ways people have been touched by Rachel's message. And whenever I speak, I hear more of these stories from young people, parents, and others who tell me about how Rachel's example has served as a kind of spark in their own lives.

My purpose in writing *Rachel Smiles* is not to hold Rachel up as someone who was sinless or ought to be worshiped. Those who knew her best know that she wasn't perfect, and Rachel repeatedly acknowledged this obvious fact in her own journals.

Rather, the reason I am writing this book is to show that even flawed and imperfect people can do great things. I am writing to bear witness to the thousands of lives that have been transformed by her message and to share some of many the stories I have heard along the way.

Sometimes it's the little things in life that can make a big difference, and that has certainly been the case with Rachel. Tragedy has transformed an unknown young woman who was deeply devoted to God and who had a strong sense of personal destiny into a symbol of hope and inspiration for many. Her faithfulness in the small things of life has brought unimagined results, and I want to share some of these with you.

In the pages that follow, you will see how something horrible has, with God's help, yielded a harvest of healing and hope.

As you read these stories, I pray that you will find encouragement for your own life. As you see how one person's service to God has created so many good things, I pray that you will be challenged to find your own ways to serve God with the gifts and talents He has given you.

And as you see how the tragedy of Columbine has been transformed into a triumph of God's will, I pray that you will have your eyes opened to the unimaginable possibilities that stretch out before you in the next moment, tomorrow, and for the rest of your life.

{ **Part 1** }

One

A Look Back in Time

I could hardly believe my eyes! I was absolutely stunned by the illustration staring up at me from the last page of my daughter's diary. Rachel Joy Scott, my seventeen-year-old, had drawn the picture just thirty minutes before she was brutally gunned down at Columbine High School on April 20, 1999. The reason for my amazement was because I had received a phone call one week earlier from a total stranger living over a thousand miles away who had described the picture I was looking at, in detail. There was absolutely no way that Frank Amedia, the man who called me, could have known what Rachel had drawn in her diary just a half hour before she was murdered!

Let me back up a little and begin with the story of the worst day of my life. April 20, 1999 began as a beautiful, sunny day in the Denver metro area. I had taken a trip over to Aurora, where I was browsing in an antique mall when I received a call from my wife, Sandy. She had heard that there had been a shooting at Columbine High School, where Rachel and my son Craig both attended. I also had a niece and nephew, Jeff and Sarah Scott, who were there.

I immediately rushed out to my pickup truck and headed toward the school. I flipped on the radio and soon realized that this was much worse than I had first imagined. I thought that perhaps someone had taken a gun to school and accidentally shot it, or at worst, that a student had shot at a teacher or another student out of personal revenge. But as I listened to the frantic description of the massacre that was unfolding, my heart started pounding out of sheer terror. The radio announcer was sobbing as he announced that there were perhaps as many as twenty-five people killed and dozens more wounded!

Rachel's Tears describes the events that unfolded over the next hours and days—days of incredible pain and sorrow, of sleepless nights, and dry, heaving sobs that continued far after the puddles of tears were exhausted.

As the initial shock began to subside, our family began to discover things about Rachel through her drawings, poems, and writings that confirmed what we already knew about her, and this gave new depth and meaning to her precious life. One of the things we found in her diaries (she had six) was a picture she had drawn several weeks before she died.

It was a sketch of a cross with the words *Jesus Christ* written in the

center. In the background was the fish symbol of Christianity. However, the thing that really captured our attention was the verse of Scripture she had chosen to quote in the picture. It said, "Greater love hath no man than this, that a man lay down his life for his friends" (John 15:13 KJV).

What we didn't pay a lot of attention to was the right side of the picture, where she had drawn a rose. There were two things that were very unusual about the rose. First, it was dripping with drops of blood; and second, it was growing not from the ground, but out of another flower—a Columbine plant! Later this portion of the picture would bring a great sense of closure to our grieving family.

After Rachel's death, everything changed. Things that seemed so important to me no longer held my interest, and things that had seemed trivial were now of utmost importance. Then came a phone call that was the beginning of a major shift in the direction of my life.

The Dream and the Drawing

Frank Amedia, a total stranger, called with an incredible story. Frank was a successful businessman living with his family in Ohio. He had seen Rachel's funeral on CNN a month earlier. He said, "Mr. Scott, you don't know me, and you'll probably think I'm crazy when I tell you why I called, but I have had a recurring dream about your daughter over the last two weeks, and I had to see if the dream meant anything to you or any other members of Rachel's family."

Frank continued, "In my dream I see a stream of tears flowing from Rachel's eyes, and they are watering something. However, I can't see what the tears are watering. I'm calling just to see if my dream would have any meaning to you or your family."

I said, "Frank, I'm sorry, but your dream doesn't mean anything to me." Frank pleaded with me to write down his phone number and call him if the dream ever came to have meaning for us, and I told him I would. After a couple of days I had forgotten all about his phone call.

Seven days after Frank's phone call I received a call from the sheriff's office. They told me that I could come pick up the contents of her backpack, which was being held as evidence. There were a number of bullet holes through the pack, and the sheriff's department had been tracing the source of each one. I rushed over immediately and took several of her schoolbooks and her two final diaries out to my truck. One of those diaries had a bullet hole through it at the spot where she had written these words: "I WON'T BE LABELED AS AVERAGE."

On the front of this diary she had written: "I WRITE, NOT FOR THE SAKE OF SUCCESS, NOT FOR THE SAKE OF FAME, NOT FOR THE SAKE OF GLORY, BUT FOR THE SAKE OF MY SOUL, RACHEL JOY."

But it was when I turned to the last page of her final diary that I was stunned! I was looking at a picture she drew just minutes before she was murdered. It was a drawing of her eyes shedding tears that were watering a rose—the same rose that she had drawn in an earlier picture, that rose dripping with drops of blood and growing out of a Columbine flower.

I counted the clear tears falling from her eyes before they touched the rose and turned to drops of blood. There were thirteen tears! Within two hours of her drawing this picture, thirteen people had been brutally gunned down by the two killers!

Suddenly the dream that Frank Amedia had described to me had become more like a prophetic message. As I looked at the drawing with the rose growing out of the Columbine plant, I had a strong sense that the Lord was saying that out of this tragedy (the Columbine plant) He would raise up a remnant

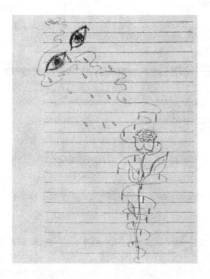

of this generation (the rose) that He would anoint with His own tears. I knew that the loss of these thirteen lives would not be in vain. More than a year later, I would learn that the rose is America's official national flower.

The other thing that impressed me as I looked at her drawing was the Bible verse she had chosen to link the two pictures together: "Greater love hath no man than this, that a man lay down his life for his friends" (John 15:13 KJV). I sat there in my truck that day with tears streaming down my face, but with the seeds of hope in my heart that something prophetically powerful and wonderful just might emerge out of something so terribly horrific.

I knew that there was a message being left for us, perhaps without Rachel's conscious knowledge. I don't believe Rachel had any idea that there would be a horrible tragedy occurring in which she and twelve others would be murdered that day. However, I do believe that God allowed her to have a sense of her own purpose and destiny.

A New Perspective

One of the first places I spoke at after Rachel's death was in Jackson, Tennessee. The owner of the Old Country Store (a prototype for the Cracker Barrels across the nation) provided an outdoor meeting place where several thousand people gathered on a hot July afternoon. I told the story of a stranger's phone call and Rachel's picture of her tears.

Darrell Speaking to Crowd

As I described Rachel's drawing and Frank's dream, a young girl near the front of the crowd burst into tears. When I finished speaking she rushed up to me and said, "Mr. Scott, I had no idea that your daughter had drawn a picture about her eyes and tears, but several nights ago I was reading my Bible and I felt strongly impressed to share some Scriptures with you that I was reading. I didn't know why I felt that way at the time, but now I do."

"Your Work Will Be Rewarded!"

This young girl handed me her Bible, which was open to Jeremiah 31:15:

> A loud voice was heard; Rachel weeping for her children and refusing to be comforted, because her children have died. Thus says the LORD, "Stop your weeping and dry your tears, for *your work will be rewarded*. I shall return the children from the land of bondage and bring them back to the land of their inheritance." (paraphrase; emphasis mine)

Now, I know that Jeremiah didn't write that passage with my daughter in mind. In fact, that prophecy was fulfilled twice in Scripture. However, that passage brought great comfort to my heart. Especially the part that reads, "Once again, the Lord was bringing comfort from His word to my grieving heart. If you allow God to do so, He will always transform your sorrow into joy." It was as though the Lord was assuring me that Rachel's death would not be in vain.

I would be reminded of that Scripture from Jeremiah one year later when Mrs. Carruthers, one of Rachel's teachers, shared this story with me.

She said, "Twenty minutes before Rachel died, I saw her drawing the picture of her eyes, the tears, and the rose. When I asked her about it, she just looked at me and said, 'Oh, Mrs. Carruthers, it isn't finished,' and then she said the strangest thing. She said, 'Mrs. Carruthers, I'm going to have an impact on the world!' And then the bell rang and I said, 'I'll see you tomorrow, Rachel,' and I watched her walk off to lunch, not realizing that I would be one of the last people to see her alive."

I was to hear those verses from Jeremiah 31:15-17 read once again, following the horrible terrorist attacks of September 11, 2001. Kirby-Jon Caldwell, the minister who had prayed at President George W. Bush's inauguration, quoted those same verses in the memorial service that was broadcast around the world in honor of the victims of that tragedy.

Rachel's drawing of her eyes, tears, and the rose, coupled with Frank Amedia's dream would prompt the writing of the best-seller *Rachel's Tears*. Millions of lives would be touched and untold thousands of hearts changed as a result of her life and death. In the end, Rachel's tears would be turned into smiles!

Two

A Chain Reaction Begins

The events of the past three years have flown by so quickly that at times I feel I have been living in the center of a hurricane. Inwardly, I have experienced horrible grief, surprising joy, and a range of other emotions that have sometimes overwhelmed my ability to process them. Outwardly, I have been before millions of people, and it seems I've passed through just as many airports and hotels.

These travels have taken me to places I never thought I would visit, and they have also given me the stories that make up the bulk of this book.

If you are familiar with the portions of Rachel's story told in the previous two books, you probably already understand much of what I am going to say in this chapter. But if you aren't, I think it would be helpful for me to explain how we have gotten from the tragedy of Columbine to the growing grassroots movement that tragedy has inspired.

A Moment in the National Spotlight

In the wake of Columbine, families of the thirteen people who died there were thrown into a confusing and tumultuous period of private grief and public attention.

Throughout the country, many people were quick to make judgments about why Columbine had happened and equally quick to announce their plan for making sure such a tragedy never happened again. One of the solutions some people proposed was stricter gun-control measures.

Clearly, if Eric Harris and Dylan Klebold, the two young men who carried out the Columbine killings, had been armed with slingshots and spitwads rather than guns and bombs, they would have caused less damage and death. After the killings, some Columbine parents became national spokespeople for various anti-gun efforts.

As for me, I am no great fan of guns. I don't even own a gun. But I believe the causes of school killings are much deeper than guns. These causes go to the soul of our nation's troubled young people, not the equipment they use to work out their despair and rage.

About a month after the killings, I was invited to Washington, D.C., to speak at a hearing of the U.S. House of Representatives judiciary committee. Here's part of what I told the committee that day:

Descendants of Cain

Since the dawn of creation there have been both good and evil in the hearts of men and women. We all contain the seeds of kindness or the seeds of violence.

The death of my wonderful daughter, Rachel Joy Scott, and the deaths of that heroic teacher and the other eleven children must not be in vain. Their blood cries out for answers.

The first recorded act of violence in human history was when Cain slew his brother Abel out in a field. The villain was not the club he used. Neither was it the NCA, the National Club Association. The true killer was Cain, and the reason for the murder could only be found in Cain's heart.

I am not a member of the NRA. I am not a hunter. I do not even own a gun. I am not here to represent or defend the NRA, but I don't believe that they are responsible for my daughter's death. If I believed they had anything to do with Rachel's murder, I would be their strongest opponent.

I am here today to declare that Columbine was not just a tragedy—it was a spiritual event that should force us to look at where the real blame lies.

Much of the blame lies here in this room. Much of that blame lies behind the pointing fingers of the accusers themselves. I wrote a poem four nights ago, before I knew I would be speaking here today, that expresses my feelings best:

> Your laws ignore our deepest needs
> Your words are empty air
> You've stripped away our heritage
> You've outlawed simple prayer
> Now gunshots fill our classrooms and precious children die
> You seek for answers everywhere
> And ask the question "Why?"
> You regulate restrictive laws
> Through legislative creed
> And yet you fail to understand
> That God is what we need!

Darrell Speaking Before Congress

Spiritual influences were present within our educational system for most of our nation's history. Many of our major colleges began as theological seminaries. This is a historic fact.

What has happened to us as a nation? We have refused to honor God, and in doing so, we have opened the doors to hatred and violence . . .

I challenge every young person in America and around the world to realize that on April 20th, 1999 at Columbine High School, prayer was brought back to our schools. Do not let the many prayers offered by those students be in vain . . . My daughter's death will not be in vain. The young people of this country will not allow that to happen.

I know that not everyone agrees with the ideas I expressed that day. But before I even knew what was happening, my speech was downloaded from Web sites, e-mailed to huge numbers of people, faxed to people who didn't have e-mail, and even posted on bulletin boards in schools and offices. Almost immediately, my phone began ringing nonstop. People called to thank me for my comments and to ask me to speak to groups in their churches and their communities. I didn't know it at the time, but I was beginning a new phase of my life. I believe God was orchestrating this new phase of ministry that would take me around the world.

One of the first big speeches I gave after that was at an evangelistic youth event sponsored by the Southern Baptist Convention. Some fourteen thousand young people had come together in a park near Atlanta, where events for the recent summer Olympics had been hosted. These kids thought they were going to hear rock bands like Jars of Clay, a popular Christian group whose videos have appeared on MTV. Most of them didn't know they were also going to listen to a talk by a man named Darrell Scott—a man they'd never heard of.

To help me, I brought my sons Craig and Mike with me, along with a man named Greg Zanis. Greg is a carpenter who had heard about Columbine and had driven across the country to erect thirteen crosses on a site overlooking the school.

As Craig and I were introduced, thirteen young people marched through the crowd carrying the thirteen crosses. They slowly made their way to the front of the crowd and formed a line of crosses in front of the stage. Tears streamed from my face as I watched my son Mike carrying his sister Rachel's cross.

As I stood on the stage, I watched in humbled amazement as a multitude of teenagers began to kneel on the ground in honor of my daughter and the others who had died at Columbine. It was an overwhelming feeling to look out over this ocean of fourteen thousand young people who kneeled in total silence as they showed their heartfelt tribute to the people who perished in this catastrophe.

Everyone knows that teenagers are synonymous with noise. They have so much energy and excitement that it's often impossible to get them to quiet down for even a second. But here on this warm summer evening, I saw a huge crowd become so hushed that I could hear a gentle wind blowing pieces of paper on the ground. I could hear birds chirping from trees in the distance. That awed silence was something I will never forget! Both Craig and I spoke that evening, and after we finished, a long line of young people formed to shake our hands and vow that Rachel's death would not be in vain. I didn't know it at the time, but this eventful evening was to be the beginning of something that would grow and grow until it reached around the world.

A Startling Discovery

Meanwhile, back in Denver, another major piece of the puzzle unexpectedly fell into place a few weeks after Rachel's death. As part of the grieving process families go through after they have lost a loved one, we were sorting through some of the things in Rachel's room. Her basement room was small, and it was crammed full by a bed, a desk, a dresser, candles, stuffed animals, photos of friends, posters from the school play she had starred in a week before her death, and other assorted mementos and remnants of a life cut short.

We had already discovered and begun to read Rachel's journals, which consisted of various notebooks and blank books where she poured her thoughts, her observations about life, and her prayers. As I was rooting around under her bed, I found two sheets of paper stapled together that had evidently slipped out of one of her school notebooks and come to rest on the carpet where no one could see them.

I had spent much of the day with Rachel's sister Bethanee, and the two of us had been weeping together as we shared memories of Rachel while looking at items she had left behind in the small sanctuary of her room.

My Ethics, My Codes of Life
Rachel Scott period 5

[handwritten margin notes: you express yourself w/ a sense of voice and originality — solid organization as well — enjoyed reading this!]

Ethics vary with environment, circumstances, and culture. In my own life, ethics play a major role. Whether it was because of the way I was raised, the experiences I've had, or just my outlook on the world and the way things should be. My biggest aspects of ethics include being honest, compassionate, and looking for the best and beauty in everyone.

I have been told repeatedly that I trust people too easily, but I find that when I put my faith and trust in people when others would not dare to, they almost never betray me. I would hope that people would put that same faith in me. Trust and honesty is an investment you put in people; if you build enough trust in them and show yourself to be honest, they will do the same in you. I value honesty so much, and it is an expectation I have of myself. I will put honesty before the risk of humiliation, before selfishness, and before anything less worthy of the Gospel truth. Even in being honest and trust worthy, I do not come off cold and heartless. Compassion and honesty go hand in hand, if enough of each is put into every situation. I admire those who trust and are trust worthy.

Compassion is the greatest form of love humans have to offer. According to Webster's Dictionary compassion means a feeling of sympathy for another's misfortune. My definition of compassion is forgiving, loving, helping, leading, and showing mercy for others. I have this theory that if one person can go out of their way to show compassion, then it will start a chain reaction of the same. People will never know how far a little kindness can go.

It wasn't until recently that I learned that the first and the second and the third impressions can be deceitful of what kind of person someone is. For example, imagine you had just met someone, and you speak with them three times on brief everyday conversations. They come off as a harsh, cruel, stubborn, and ignorant person. You reach your judgment based on just these three encounters. Let me ask you something...did you ever ask them what their goal in life is, what kind of past they came from, did they experience love, did they experience hurt, did you look into their soul and not just at their appearance? Until you know them and not just their "type," you have no right to shun them. You have not looked for their beauty, their good. You have not seen the light in their eyes. Look hard enough and you will always find a light, and you can even help it grow, if you don't walk away from those three impressions first.

I am sure that my codes of life may be very different from yours, but how do you know that trust, compassion, and beauty will not make this world a better place to be in and this life a better one to live? My codes may seem like a fantasy that can never be reached, but test them for yourself, and see the kind of effect they have in the lives of people around you. You just may start a chain reaction.

15

Now we were looking at another personal memento. We wondered what insight it would yield into the heart of the wonderful young woman whose absence we felt so strongly.

The two-page paper was actually an essay entitled, "My Ethics, My Codes of Life." The author was "Rachel Scott, period 5." The upper right-hand corner of the front page indicated that the paper had earned top grades—25 points out of a possible 25 points—and it featured these words in her teacher's pretty handwriting: "You express yourself w/a sense of voice and originality—solid organization as well. I enjoyed reading this."

As we sat down on the corner of Rachel's bed to read the essay, we were both struck by what it had to say:

School assignments rarely become the basis of great literature. Many students dash off essays quickly, but this paper seemed to be more thoughtful than some I have seen. Even more, the paper provided another in a series of revelations about the sister and daughter Bethanee and I were missing so much. Here, in a simple essay of about five hundred words, Rachel had clearly summed up her approach to life, evident in so much of what she had done while she was alive.

I read and reread this brief essay through the tears that were flooding my eyes. As I did so, I began to see the outlines of an idea that I could pass on to some of the young people and others I was speaking to. And so, in *Chain Reaction* we developed Rachel's ideas more fully, paying special attention to the five key values that were the core of her convictions: forgiving, loving, helping, leading, and showing mercy.

If you go to a big bookstore and peruse the self-help section, you may find hundreds of volumes that tell readers how to be more successful, how to earn more money, how to have firmer stomachs, and how to make people like you. But in all the books of this type I've ever seen, I don't think any of them have ever offered a more profound and powerful set of values than the five simple concepts Rachel made the foundation of her own code of ethics.

When I spoke to audiences about these values, the response was amazing. Of course, people want to honor and remember the tragedy of Columbine, as the fourteen thousand young people had done in Atlanta. But people also need a message of hope and purpose that could help them transcend the horrors of violence and death. Instead of merely looking back at Columbine and shedding a tear of sadness, people wanted to know what lessons could be learned from this tragic episode.

As I offered Rachel's values to the people who invited me to speak to them, I found that the concepts of forgiving, loving, helping, leading, and showing mercy could not only encourage people and give them inspiration; even more, these ideas would soon become the basis of thousands of selfless acts that are described later in this book.

Another Death, Another Book

The more I have thought about these things, the more I have been struck by the similarities between Rachel's life and the experience of another teenage girl who died under horrific circumstances, but who left behind a record of her life in private journals she had kept.

I am thinking of Anne Frank, whose *Diary of a Young Girl* was published exactly fifty years before I am writing these words. Anne Frank died in the Holocaust, one of the most horrible single events in the history of the human race. I don't want to compare the death of an estimated six million Jews and other innocent victims to the deaths of one teacher and twelve students at Columbine. On the other hand, evil is evil, no matter how many people are involved. And I see profound parallels between these two tragedies that are separated by decades but are united by threads of horror and hope.

Anne Frank was born into a Jewish family in Frankfurt, Germany, on June 12, 1929. Five years later, her family moved to Amsterdam. It was there that Anne received a diary as a present for her thirteenth birthday.

In 1942, the family went into hiding in a desperate attempt to avoid being rounded up by the Nazis. For the next two years, Anne wrote down everything that happened to her in her diary. As one writer put it, "She became the most memorable figure to emerge from World War II—besides Hitler, of course, who also proclaimed his life and his beliefs in a book."

As Anne wrote her thoughts in her book, she developed a relationship with her journal that was similar in some respects to the way Rachel felt about her own journals. "I hope that you will be a great support and comfort to me," she wrote in her beloved book. "I want to be useful or give pleasure to people around me who yet don't really know me. I want to go on living even after my death!"

During the two years that Anne, her sister, and her mother and father hid from the Nazis, she poured her heart into her words. One moving passage records her search for meaning at a time when evil seemed to be winning:

> I simply can't build up my hopes on a foundation consisting of confusion, misery and death. I see the world gradually being turned into a wilderness; I hear the ever approaching thunder, which will destroy us too; I can feel the sufferings of millions; and yet, if I look up into the heavens, I think that it will all come right, that this cruelty will end, and that peace and tranquillity will return again.
>
> I must uphold my ideals, for perhaps the time will come when I shall be able to carry them out.

In both the case of Rachel and the case of Anne Frank, young girls looked at the world around them and were saddened by what they saw. But rather than giving up hope, they knew they must cling ever more tightly to the values and beliefs that gave their lives shape and meaning.

You and I probably wouldn't have ever heard of Anne Frank if she had lived to be eighty years old, been married, and had children and a garden. Unfortunately, she and so many other children never got that chance. Anne Frank died a horrible death from typhus in the Bergen-Belsen concentration camp in 1945. Two years later, her father Otto, who miraculously survived, published *Anne Frank: The Diary of a Young Girl*, and people young and old have been reading about the faith and courage of this remarkable girl ever since. Likewise, you probably wouldn't have heard of people named Rachel Scott or Darrell Scott if it weren't for Columbine. But God has made our world in such a way that horror and hope coexist.

There are certainly occasions when it seems that horror will win the day. Frankly, that was the way I felt at times in the aftermath of Rachel's death. But as we will see in the next chapter, hope has not yet given in and declared defeat.

And thankfully, even the most unimaginable disasters can give birth to a new and even more powerful promise of a brighter tomorrow.

Whom will you serve?

At sixty years old, Bob Dylan is even older than I am, but he is still making records, winning Grammy Awards, and as I write, planning yet another summer concert tour.

During much of the 1960s and 1970s, Bob Dylan was the voice of an entire generation. His songs explored war, death, racism, sexism, hypocrisy, poverty, and so many of the other issues that helped define an era. Then in 1979, Dylan came out with an album that shocked his millions of fans. The album was called *Slow Train Coming*, and it would be the first of three records that revealed the poet/musician's passionate faith in Jesus.

One of the songs on *Slow Train Coming* was a provocative number entitled "Gotta Serve Somebody." Verse after verse, the song described the various decisions people must make during the course of their lives. After rehearsing various complex ethical dilemmas, Dylan's nasal voice rang out the song's central message in a memorable chorus:

> It may be the Devil
> Or it may be the Lord
> But you gotta serve somebody.

In many ways, this song summarizes the main reason I have spent much of the last three years encouraging people to embrace Rachel's values and put them into action.

We are all born into a world that offers us a dizzying variety of choices, and day by day, we are forced to navigate our way through the maze by doing our best to make the right decisions. The decisions we make will ultimately be based on what we believe. For those who don't know what they believe, their decisions will reflect that uncertainty.

But for me, a major part of what motivated me to devote my time to spreading Rachel's message was the conviction that if I didn't, another set of values would win the day. This was a set of values espoused by the two young men who killed Rachel and twelve others that day in 1999.

Chain Reactions of Two Kinds

Rachel wrote her essay about her codes of life in March 1999, one month before the Columbine tragedy. Some months after her death, I made a shocking discovery. At about the same time Rachel was writing her essay, Eric Harris, the Columbine killer who police reports say shot Rachel to death outside the school, was using a video camera to record his own much more diabolical code of ethics.

Looking straight into the camera lens and cradling one of the guns that would later cause so much death and destruction, Eric made the following statement: "We need a [expletive] kick start—we need to get a chain reaction going here! It's going to be like 'Doom' (the video game) man, after the bombs explode. That [expletive] shotgun (kisses the gun) straight out of 'Doom.'"

The parallels still amaze me. Rachel and Eric had lived in the same city. They were born just days apart. They lived in comfortable houses just miles away from each other. They had attended some of the same classes in school. And they both died at that school on April 20, 1999.

Both had recorded their respective codes of ethics just one month before their deaths. Both believed that they were supposed to start a chain reaction. Both expected that these chain reactions, if successful, would be the beginning of a whole series of later actions and reactions, on into eternity!

Eric Harris certainly started several chain reactions. Not only did he kill innocent people at Columbine High School, but he provided the inspiration for a number of "copycat" school-shooting plans over the next few years, some successful and some halted by alert students and responsive law enforcement personnel. Eric rightly predicted that people would demand stricter gun-control laws after the tragedy. His "chain reaction" caused death, suffering, mourning, anger, accusations, lawsuits, political debate, and more negative repercussions.

Meanwhile, Rachel's chain reaction, which was inspired by her own code of ethics, has created an entirely different set of results, as you will see.

Both young people knew what they wanted to do and went about doing it with all their energy. Both also said that someday, the world would know who they were. The question all of us need to think about is this: What kind of chain reaction will our lives inspire?

Choose Whom You Will Serve

I am reminded of the words of Joshua, a military and spiritual leader who led the nation of Israel into a land called Palestine and helped transform it into the "promised land."

Joshua was a brilliant strategist and an admired leader, but there was one problem that plagued him at nearly every step he took. The people he was leading were disobedient and double-minded. They said they wanted to serve God, but when things got tough they rebelled, falling into idolatry and sin.

In the closing chapter of the Old Testament Book of Joshua, this man of God issues a challenge to the nation he leads:

> Now fear the LORD and serve him with all faithfulness. Throw away the gods your forefathers worshiped beyond the River and in Egypt, and serve the LORD. But if serving the LORD seems undesirable to you, then choose for yourselves this day whom you will serve, whether the gods your forefathers served beyond the River, or the gods of the Amorites, in whose land you are living. But as for me and my household, we will serve the LORD. (Joshua 24:14-15)

Does serving God seem undesirable to you? And who is being served in your household? I don't know about you, but I have chosen to serve God. And for now, a major part of that service involves talking to people like you and challenging you to do the same thing. The way you serve God won't be the same way I do it, or the same way that Rachel did it. God has His own plans and dreams for you and the rest of your life.

But right now, as your eyes reach the bottom of this page, decide whom you will serve. Only after doing that can you determine what kind of chain reaction you can jump-start with your own life.

Three

Seeds of Hope

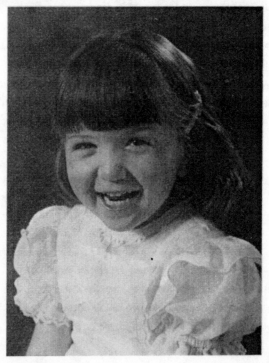

In an article published in April 2001—the second anniversary of the killings at Columbine—the *Tampa Tribune* described some of the many ways the tragedy had helped inspire a spiritual awakening among students at many schools.

The Columbine High School massacre extinguished many lives, the newspaper said, but the tragedy has motivated teens, including many from nonchurch backgrounds, to become more proactive and bold on campus about their faith.

"I truly think it lit a fire in a lot of kids," said Wendy Murray Zoba, a writer for *Christianity Today* and the author of the book *Day of Reckoning: Columbine and the Search for America's Soul.* "It put life into their spiritual longings. They consider those murdered students to be martyrs, and they don't want their deaths to be in vain."

Although school violence has continued around the country, the paper reported that more young people are turning to God to impact their schools. A record number of students are using Christian activism to stop school violence by forming campus prayer groups and Bible studies.

The article included comments from Kathy Conner, a Young Life director in Florida. Conner said her ministry had grown in three years from five schools and about 400 students to seven schools and 850 students in one Florida county. She said that since Columbine, she had witnessed a "huge hunger" for meaning and significance on the part of these young people.

The paper also described the work of Gaither High School seniors Robyn French and Ali Lombardi, both eighteen, who had organized a Christian concert at their Tampa school to commemorate Columbine and inspire fellow students. "I know that the lifestyle my generation is leading is going to destroy them," said Lombardi. "Jesus gives you a purpose. Without a purpose, you can lead a destructive life."

The article said other teens had been emboldened and energized to stand up for their faith since Columbine. More than thirty thousand teens from across Florida filled Tropicana Field in St. Petersburg for a two-day event sponsored by Teen Mania Ministries, a Texas-based nonprofit youth missions organization. The event was designed to inspire teens to be peer leaders in their schools, the *Tribune* reported. And nationwide, the article noted an increased number of students participating in the annual "See You at the Pole" prayer rally sponsored on school grounds. From 1990 (when the event started) to 2001, participation had increased from forty-five thousand to more than three million students.

Stories like these are being reported from all over the country and the world as young people have found spiritual inspiration and motivation for a deeper dedication from the death and destruction that terrorized Columbine. Some people are confused by this. They don't understand how something so good can come out of something so bad. But Christians who serve a crucified and resurrected Christ know that the message of their faith contains powerful seeds of hope.

These seeds of hope give them the supernatural power that enables them to transcend tragedy and transform sorrow into joy. Or, as British writer G. K. Chesterton once put it: "Hope means expectancy when things are otherwise hopeless."

Understanding what the Bible teaches us about seeds of hope is essential for understanding what has happened in the three years since Columbine became a front-page story. And beyond that understanding the Christian basis of hope will help us live our lives more fully and more devotedly.

Harvesting Hope

As I read the New Testament Gospels of Matthew, Mark, Luke, and John, I am continually amazed at how Jesus' disciples just didn't get it. Jesus had gone out into the world and recruited a group of twelve key disciples to join His mission to save the world. "Come follow me," He commanded them. And they did.

But as this ragtag group of fishermen, tax collectors, and other ordinary people walked with Jesus, ate with Him, and listened to Him as He taught the curious multitudes, they repeatedly failed to grasp some of the central themes of His teaching.

The disciples were particularly dense when it came to understanding the central fact of Jesus' ministry on earth: that He must die and three days later rise from the dead. Only by His death and resurrection would He complete the work His heavenly Father had given Him and provide us with a way to be cleansed from our sins and experience fellowship with the almighty God. He repeatedly made statements such as "And I, if I be lifted up from the earth, will draw all men unto me" (John 12:32 KJV) and would explain that this signified His death and resurrection. He talked to them about the Good Shepherd laying down His life for His sheep and yet they chose to ignore the sometimes subtle, sometimes blatant attempts to prepare them for His crucifixion and death. Take, for example, this statement He made in the Gospel of John: "The hour has come for the Son of Man to be glorified. I tell you the truth, unless a kernel of wheat falls to the ground and dies, it remains only a single seed. But if it dies, it produces many seeds" (John 12:23-24).

Often when Jesus was trying to explain complex spiritual concepts to earthly-minded listeners, He would use powerful examples from the natural world that had been created by His Father. Today, many of us have less contact with nature than we do with computers, televisions, air-conditioned buildings, or shopping malls. But in Jesus' day, people were much more closely tied to the natural world. Aside from this, the way nature works is many times a particularly good reflection of the kingdom workings of God. So when He wanted to make an important point, Jesus turned to nature for illustrations.

His parable of the sower and the seed uses the simple example of planting seeds to explain the mystery of why some people's faith grows strong while others fall away. Seed that grows in fertile soil produces deep roots and much fruit. On the other hand, seed that falls on rocky ground, where it can't grow and is soon choked out, quickly dies off.

On another occasion, Jesus explained the relationship between good and evil by talking about the wheat and the tares, or weeds. Why doesn't God simply destroy all the weeds with some kind of heavenly weed-whacker? His simpleminded disciples asked. If that happened, said Jesus, some of the good wheat would be destroyed in the process. It would be better to let both grow until the final judgment day, when God will be able to separate out the good from the bad.

In case after case, Jesus turned to natural examples like these to illustrate supernatural truths. He does so again in the passage about the seed of wheat, where He says it must fall to the ground and die before it can bring forth new life. I don't know about you, but I would rather live than die; I think most people feel that way. Jesus' disciples certainly did.

But Jesus had a clearer picture of His mission and a higher understanding of the relationship between life and death. Jesus understood that death was not the end, but only the beginning. He also understood that He had come to do the will of His Father, not His own will. It was God's purpose that Christ was to suffer and die in our place. Jesus submitted to that purpose even though He knew the price that He must pay for obedience. He prayed, "My Father, if it is possible, may this cup (of suffering and death) be taken from me," and then He expressed an obedient heart when He continued, "Yet not as I will, but as you will" (Matthew 26:39).

Sometimes God's purposes cannot immediately be seen, and sometimes they won't be seen in this life. However, we can be assured that in everything He does have a purpose that will ultimately make sense to us all in the light of eternity. Sometimes even death becomes a catalyst to life.

If Jesus had been able to choose what He wanted to do, perhaps He would have chosen to remain a simple carpenter rather than accepting God's call on His life to be the Savior of all humanity. But Jesus accepted God's call and submitted His will to God's will. In doing so, He saw that He must die in order for us to live.

The students who were killed at Columbine didn't want to die, although as we've seen, Rachel anticipated that she didn't have long to live. Still, we can now see that in the three years since that tragedy, their deaths have brought new life to many.

Those of us who have read the Bible and begun to grasp its message shouldn't be surprised by this. As Jesus so clearly illustrated, death often contains the seeds of hope.

Called to Die

"When Christ calls a man, he bids him come and die."

Those words were written by Dietrich Bonhoeffer, a German pastor, theologian, teacher, and writer. He wrote a book called *The Cost of Discipleship* that is widely regarded as one of the most influential and important books of the twentieth century.

At the time he wrote these words, Bonhoeffer probably wasn't thinking about physical death, but rather the "death to self" that the Bible teaches is the norm for all serious Christians. But soon it became obvious to

Bonhoeffer that if he was to apply his theology to the realities of daily life in Nazi-controlled Germany, his physical death would probably follow.

His boldness, bravery, and radical Christian commitment made him a hero of the faith, and today, his legacy continues to inspire new generations of Christians to give their all for God. I am including an overview of his life in this chapter because learning more about his life will help all of us understand the types of Christian commitment that may be needed in a post-Columbine era.

A Faithful Man in Faithless Times

Bonhoeffer was born in 1906 and was raised in a devout and godly home. By the time he was fourteen, he knew he wanted to be a theologian. Nine years later, he was teaching theology at Berlin University.

Then in 1933, a man named Adolf Hitler became Germany's chancellor and promoted a political philosophy called Nazism. Many Germans, including the majority of German Christians, hailed Hitler as a strong and powerful leader. But Bonhoeffer saw things differently. During a 1933 broadcast on a Berlin radio station, he boldly called Hitler a "misleader."

From that day on Bonhoeffer was labeled an enemy of the state. He became a member of an underground Christian movement and taught at a seminary that operated outside of government control. It was while he was teaching that he delivered the lectures that would become the basis of *The Cost of Discipleship*. In one of the most famous passages from that book, Bonhoeffer condemns something he calls "cheap grace":

Cheap grace is the deadly enemy of our Church. We are fighting today for costly grace.

Cheap grace is the preaching of forgiveness without requiring repentance, baptism without Church discipline, Communion without confession, absolution without personal confession. Cheap grace is grace without discipleship, grace without the cross, grace without Jesus Christ, living and incarnate.

Costly grace is the treasure hidden in the field; for the sake of it a man will gladly go and sell all that he has. It is the pearl of great price to buy for which the merchant will sell all his goods. It is the kingly rule of Christ, for whose sake a man will pluck out the eye which causes him to stumble, it is the call of Jesus Christ at which the disciple leaves his nets and follows him.

Costly grace is the gospel which must be sought again and again, the gift which must be asked for, the door at which a man must knock.

Such grace is costly because it calls us to follow, and it is grace because it calls us to follow Jesus Christ. It is costly because it costs a man his life, and it is grace because it gives a man the only true life. It is costly because it condemns sin, and grace because it justifies the sinner. Above all, it is costly because it cost God the life of his Son: "ye were bought at a price," and what has cost God much cannot be cheap for us. Above all, it is grace because God did not reckon his Son too dear a price to pay for our life, but delivered him up for us. Costly grace is the Incarnation of God.

Costly grace is the sanctuary of God; it has to be protected from the world, and not thrown to the dogs. It is therefore the living word, the Word of God, which he speaks as it pleases him. Costly grace confronts us as a gracious call to follow Jesus, it comes as a word of forgiveness to the broken spirit and the contrite heart. Grace is costly because it compels a man to submit to the yoke of Christ and follow him; it is grace because Jesus says: "My yoke is easy and my burden is light."

Although I may not agree with every detail of Bonhoeffer's theology, I agree with the spirit of what he is expressing here. Passages like this made Bonhoeffer an international celebrity. He traveled to the United States in 1939 for a lecture tour and received many offers to stay in the U.S. instead of returning to the growing confusion in his native land. But Bonhoeffer felt a strong calling to return: "I shall have no right to participate in the reconstruction of Christian life in Germany after the war if I do not share in the trials of this time with my people."

He returned to Germany, but as the Third Reich became increasingly powerful, Bonhoeffer became a member of the underground resistance movement that actively worked to overthrow the Nazi government. At the same time, he tried to go on with life, and in January 1943, he became engaged to be married. But his marriage would never happen. Bonhoeffer and others who had plotted against the Nazis were arrested and imprisoned.

Conditions in prison were horrible, but even there, Bonhoeffer was able to find hope in the midst of despair. As he wrote in one of his many letters from prison: "I believe that God can and will bring good out of evil, even out of the greatest evil. Much as I long to be out of here, I don't believe a single day has been wasted. What will come out of my time here it is still too early to say, but something will come of it."

Bonhoeffer thought he might die at any moment, but at the same time he hoped he would survive. But isn't that the way life is for all of us? Who among us knows how long we will live or what we will be able to do during the remaining days we have? Here's how he expressed that tension: "There remains for us only the very narrow way, often extremely difficult to find, of living every day as if it were our last, and yet living in faith and responsibility as though there were to be a great future."

And although his circumstances certainly gave him plenty to complain about, he kept his eyes on God, who had called him and sustained him throughout his life: "I am traveling with gratitude and cheerfulness along the road where I am being led."

Bonhoeffer continued to hope that he would be released, but on Sunday, April 8, 1945, he was leading a prison church service when he was interrupted by two German officials. "Come with us," they said. The next day, Bonhoeffer was executed. Only three days later, Allied troops liberated the prison and freed those who were still alive.

More than half a century later, people are still praising the German pastor who stood up to the Nazis. One historian said this: "Dietrich Bonhoeffer's life and death left a clear legacy for subsequent generations of Christians. From his shining example we learn that spiritual power will surely prevail over the forces of evil—but we must take an active part in that struggle." At a time when the battle between good and evil seems to be intensifying, this one loyal believer's example serves as a challenge to us all.

Matters of Life and Death

Few of us will ever face the kinds of horrific challenges Bonhoeffer faced, but he was right when he said, "When Christ calls a man, he bids him come and die." We may not hear sentiments like this expressed very often in Sunday sermons or in popular Christian books, but even the briefest review of the words of Jesus will turn up many direct comments about how our lives are no longer our own once we have given them over to Christ's Lordship.

In the tenth chapter of Matthew, Jesus talks to His twelve disciples before sending them out to minister in His name. Among the instructions He gives is this passage about life and death:

> Do not be afraid of those who kill the body but cannot kill the soul. Rather, be afraid of the One who can destroy both soul and body in hell. Are not two sparrows sold for a penny? Yet not one of them will fall to the ground apart from the will of your Father. And even the very hairs of your head are all numbered. So don't be afraid; you are worth more than many sparrows. (Matt. 10:28-31)

A few verses later, Jesus tells His disciples to count the cost of serving Him. "Anyone who loves his father or mother more than me is not worthy of me; anyone who loves his son or daughter more than me is not worthy of me; and anyone who does not take his cross and follow me is not worthy of me. Whoever finds his life will lose it, and whoever loses his life for my sake will find it" (Matt. 10:37-39). Jesus tells the disciples it will cost them nothing short of their entire lives to follow Him, but He promises that they will find their true lives by doing so.

Jesus returns to the idea of taking up our crosses in Matthew 16. The time of His own death is growing closer, and He is explaining to His disciples in greater detail what this will entail—for Him and for them. "If anyone would come after me, he must deny himself and take up his cross and follow me. For whoever wants to save his life will lose it, but whoever loses his life for me will find it" (Matt. 16:24-25).

In Luke 12, we find Jesus exploring similar themes in a slightly different way. After teaching the multitudes with a variety of parables, Jesus turns to his disciples and says, "Therefore I tell you, do not worry about your life, what you will eat; or about your body, what you will wear. Life is more than food, and the body more than clothes" (Luke 12:22-23). He goes on to talk about the birds of the air and the lilies of the field. God cares for all of these aspects of His creation, says Jesus. And if He cares so much for these things, imagine how much He cares for us. Therefore, we should not worry about our lives, but entrust them to His care.

In John's Gospel, Jesus teaches His disciples even more about His sacrificial love. "I am the good shepherd; I know my sheep and my sheep know me—just as the Father knows me and I know the Father—and I lay down my life for the sheep" (John 10:14-15). A few chapters later, Jesus challenges his disciples to do likewise. "My command is this: Love each other as I have loved you. Greater love has no one than this, that he lay down his life for his friends. You are my friends if you do what I command" (John 15:12-14).

No one asked Rachel and the others who were killed at Columbine to sacrifice their lives for others. But I wonder how they would have responded if they had been asked. Knowing what I now know about Rachel's private spiritual life and her commitment to God, I have an idea what she might have said.

What would you say if Jesus asked the same of you today?

From Happiness to Hope

If you conducted a survey of people you know and asked them what the main purpose of life is, many would respond by saying one word: happiness.

The U.S. Declaration of Independence, first read in Congress on July 4, 1776, declares: "We hold these truths to be self-evident, that all men are created equal, that they are endowed by their Creator with certain inalienable rights, that among these are life, liberty and the pursuit of happiness."

There is even a widespread idea promoted in many churches that the primary point of the Christian life is the happiness of the believer. Whether you're in a "name-it-and-claim-it" church or some other congregation that highlights the supposed benefits of the Christian life rather than its duties and responsibilities, believers often focus on what's in it for them instead of what they are called to do for Jesus' sake.

I don't know about you, but when I became a Christian as a young person, life did not suddenly become an unending succession of happy moments. Throughout life I have encountered challenges and hardships. The tragedy at Columbine was probably the most difficult experience I have ever endured, but there have been many other smaller tragedies as well.

After Rachel was killed, I certainly asked God that all-important question: Why did this happen? But I didn't blame God for the tragedy or turn my back on Him because I was suffering. The idea that Christianity equals happiness is a myth, and the sooner we get rid of it the better.

You've probably never heard of a man named Horatio G. Spafford. He lived during the nineteenth century and wrote a well-known hymn entitled "It Is Well with My Soul." (If you've never heard of it, ask your parents or a Christian who is over the age of forty-five.)

The first verse is a moving testimony of unshakable faith in God:

> When peace like a river attendeth my way,
> When sorrows like sea billows roll;
> Whatever my lot, Thou hast taught me to say,
> It is well, it is well with my soul.
> It is well with my soul,
> It is well, it is well with my soul.

One might think that Spafford was a happy-go-lucky guy who never experienced a moment of sorrow or pain, but if you study his life you find a quite different story.

Spafford had invested most of his life savings in real estate, but the Chicago fire of 1871 destroyed most of his property and left him destitute. Later, his wife and four daughters sailed to Europe. But the ship was struck by another vessel and sank in twelve minutes. All four of Spafford's daughters drowned. When she reached land in Wales, his wife sent him a sorrowful telegram: "Saved alone."

Spafford sailed to Europe to be reunited with his wife. It was while he was crossing the Atlantic Ocean and his own ship passed over the same waters where his daughters died that he wrote the words to "It Is Well with My Soul."

As I travel around the world speaking to groups about Columbine, people continually ask me how I have managed to survive the grief and sorrow of the past three years. God's grace has certainly helped me, but it has also been helpful for me to recall that the Christian life was never advertised as being happy and pain-free. Pain is a part of life, no matter whether one follows Christ or not. At least as a believer, I know I am loved by a Savior who Himself suffered for me. This is an important seed of hope in my life.

Heartbroken but Hopeful

The past three years have been difficult for me, and there have been days when I have been wracked by heartbreak and sorrow. But today, I can declare that I remain hopeful.

I have tremendous hope for the youth of today, because I don't believe that Eric Harris and Dylan Klebold represent the majority of young people. Troubled souls like these represent only a minority, and the kids I see when I speak are the majority.

I have hope because events like Columbine have shown the youth of the world that there is a deep spiritual deficiency in their lives that is forcing them to cry out for help, for truth, for a spiritual experience, and for God.

I have hope for the American nation, because tragedies like Columbine and the terrorist attacks of 9/11 have served as national wake-up calls, bringing us back to a renewed sense of God and country. I have hope for our country's leaders and for our nation's educational system because people are realizing that there must be a return to godly moral values and enduring spiritual principles.

I have hope because death precedes new life just as decaying wood from ancient oak trees provides the fertilizer for new seedlings that will grow into tomorrow's forests.

I have hope because Jesus has conquered death, and in Him, we have new life.

Like Horatio G. Spafford, I have seen my share of trouble. But like him, I can declare that "it is well with my soul."

{ **Part 2** }

Four

From Halls of Tragedy to Halls of Hope

The killings at Columbine transformed a school into a killing field. In an instant, a crowded lunchroom, a busy library, and nearby hallways and classrooms became battlegrounds where students and teachers tried to hide from killers in their midst.

In her journals, Rachel had once described the corridors of Columbine as "halls of tragedy." We believe this was one of many premonitions she had about a coming event that might result in her own death.

Today, portions of the school building have been redesigned so that the areas where most of the killing took place now have new walls, fresh paint, and big windows that let in the brightness of the sun. But it takes more than physical changes to erase the memories of April 20, 1999. That's why I am so thankful that I have been part of a growing nationwide movement called Rachel's Challenge that helps organize school assemblies in auditoriums across the country. So far we have participated in more than a hundred of these events, which feature a variety of speakers and presentations. By doing so, we are helping to spread Rachel's message and trying to transform halls of tragedy into halls of hope.

Rachel's Challenge Goes to School

Earlier, I mentioned that Rachel's sister Bethanee and I discovered one of Rachel's school essays in her bedroom shortly after her death. That essay, entitled "My Ethics, My Codes of Life" (see page 15), could have easily been overlooked or discarded because it was stuck in the bedsprings under her bed, but we found it, and we were amazed as we read its contents.

At that time, this essay was just another glimpse into Rachel's life and soul that we treasured as we mourned her passing. But over time, as more of Rachel's journals and drawings were discovered, this two-page document began to take on a greater significance in our minds. The essay was written as an English assignment, but Rachel had used this ordinary exercise as a way to try and make an impact on her surroundings.

Interestingly, Rachel's essay does not mention God or Jesus one time! That was so uncharacteristic of her, as you know if you have read anything else she has written. All of her other letters, journal entries, drawings, and papers were filled with her prayers to God or Scriptures that had special meanings to her. But in this essay, she took the biblical principles that were foundational to her faith and action and described them in general terms that different people could understand, regardless of their religious affiliations or spiritual states. There was no religious lingo or "Christian-ese" to confuse or offend people who didn't share her beliefs.

Did she somehow know that this paper was going to provide the basis for something completely different? Perhaps. And just maybe, in this essay Rachel's smile has become a mischievous grin as she translated key Christian principles in non-Christian terms that anyone can understand.

Ironically, if her paper had been filled with her characteristic references to her faith in God and her devotion to Jesus, we could have never used this document as a basis for our programs in public schools across the country. But there is not one controversial word in her essay when it comes to presenting it in public schools anywhere! Just as Jesus often used parables about farming and nature to explain complex spiritual principles, Rachel had used common language to explain the values that were the keys to her soul.

In the essay, Rachel challenges her readers to start a chain reaction of kindness and compassion and to adopt a set of values that includes honesty, compassion, and looking for the best and the beauty in everyone in their schools. The essay wasn't just a theoretical text. Rather, it was the basis of who Rachel was and how she acted at school and elsewhere. She was kind to students at Columbine who were picked on, who were ignored, and who didn't fit in with the established cliques in school. She acted on her own "Codes of Life" every day.

Kindness and compassion don't come easily for everyone, especially if these qualities aren't part of a person's life experience. But they are expressions that can be learned and appreciated. And that's what Rachel desired for everyone she encountered. Now, her challenge to a generation of students in this simple two-page essay has become a nationwide movement. Rachel's Challenge is now a national program of pro-kindness for schools that want to stem the increase in violence and bullying on their campuses.

Rachel's Challenge was developed by a team of people who seemed to come together by divine appointment. That's the only way I can describe it. The right people with the right experience and talent came together at the right time and embraced this vision of taking Rachel's simple challenge to start a chain reaction of kindness and compassion. Now students in junior high and high schools across the country are hearing and accepting the challenge that Rachel declared. And the response has been amazing. The climate on these campuses is changing.

In times like ours, I believe that every teacher, principal, or parent would be glad to support schools where these values were the norm.

Birth of a Movement

I would like to briefly explain how Rachel's Challenge was launched.

In the wake of the killings at Columbine, I knew that there were a number of survivors who had powerful stories to tell about their experiences. Many of them were friends of Rachel's and believed in her call to compassion and kindness. They wanted an outlet to tell their stories and to challenge other students to avoid creating in their own schools an atmosphere where another Columbine could happen.

Meanwhile, at one of my speaking events, I met an exciting man named Bill Sanders. Bill has been speaking on character and values to schools in the Midwest for more than twenty years. Schools regularly invite Bill to speak because of the positive impact he has on students who hear his message. As Bill and I began to talk about Rachel's challenge to her generation to start a chain reaction of kindness and compassion, Bill caught the vision for how Rachel's message could inspire this generation of students. After a time of praying and talking with his family, Bill believed God was calling him to help us start a program to take Rachel's challenge across the country.

I also had met a number of state and local school administrators in two years of speaking. When I had the opportunity to talk about Rachel's challenge to people who work in school settings, they said that if we ever developed such a program, they would gladly host it in their schools.

After Rachel's death, we had established an organization called Columbine Redemption to promote Rachel's legacy and help coordinate some of our speaking and other programs. When I presented my vision for Rachel's Challenge to our board of directors, they gladly stepped up to make the commitment to provide initial funding.

Two of our board members, Edgar and Yvonne Miles, from El Paso, Texas, went even further. They believed they could get schools in El Paso to sign on to host Rachel's Challenge, making El Paso a kind of testing ground for this new outreach.

Now, all of the essential ingredients were in place. We went to work. I recruited students to be the speakers for assemblies. Bill Sanders began writing a script and planning how to train these students to give the presentations. And Yvonne began signing up schools in El Paso. It was a massive effort, but the results went beyond our wildest dreams.

On to El Paso

The students who survived the killings at Columbine had endured more than their share of terror and nightmares. I would have understood if none of them ever wanted to think about the experience again, and instead just put it behind them and get on with their lives.

But that's not what happened. Today, I am so proud of the students who responded to my invitation to be assembly presenters in El Paso. They put aside their own fears and insecurities in order to be messengers of hope to tens of thousands of students who desperately wanted to hear what they had to say.

Here is a listing of the students who helped us out. The brief comments here fail to do justice to their contribution to that initial project, but they provide an idea of the obstacles they had to overcome in reflecting on their memories and sharing them with others:

- Sara Arzola was one of Rachel's best friends. Sara had sat next to Rachel in class just before Rachel went outside to eat lunch on April 20, 1999. It was while she was eating lunch with a friend that she was killed. Sara never saw her again.

- Nicole Nowlin is one of many Columbine students who received both emotional and physical scars that day. She was shot nine times and still carries bullet fragments in her body.

- Stephen and Jonathan Cohen are the brothers who penned "My Columbine," a tribute song that was sung at numerous memorial events. Little did they know that their song would become an unofficial anthem of the Columbine tragedy when it was broadcast worldwide on CNN and other media outlets.

- Adam Kyler is one of the students Rachel reached out to in a special way. Adam has his own unique issues and challenges, but he laid these down to speak to the students in El Paso, where he soon became the "most famous" member of our team.

- Josh Weidmann is a spiritually committed young man who became a beacon of hope for many students in the dark days after the Columbine incident.

- Scott Dodge was with a team of students involved in a ministry called First Priority. These students were in Littleton the week of the shooting, and he continues as one of our main speakers.

- My son Craig, who struggled so much for so long after Columbine, agreed to come to El Paso and share his own horrifying story. During the course of the activities in Texas, he came to fully embrace the Rachel's Challenge program.

- And finally, I must mention my daughter Dana (who is covered in another chapter of this book). As you will see, Dana has committed herself to carrying on Rachel's legacy by traveling and speaking almost as much as me. Dana has a beautiful heart that has touched so many lives in the last two years, and her participation in the events in El Paso had a powerful impact.

There were months of stress as plans moved forward and we experienced setbacks. We had never done anything of this magnitude before, but God always came through with exactly what we needed. There were volunteers to set up video projectors, drivers to take our speakers around to the schools, hotel managers who gave us rooms at the Holiday Inn for prices far below normal rates. And the wonderful people at First Baptist Church in El Paso opened their doors for planning meetings and luncheons where we recruited volunteers and churches to join the effort. As I look back at it all now, I can only conclude that there was one miracle after another that resolved problems and issues we hadn't foreseen.

I don't know why God called us to El Paso to test-drive Rachel's

Challenge, but I am grateful that's where we started. The people of that city opened their lives and hearts to our team in a fabulous way. The community's schools opened their doors to us, and we conducted forty-three assemblies in El Paso during that week, reaching more than thirty-three thousand students.

Our student presenters showed news footage from the day of the Columbine tragedy, talked about their experience at Columbine, and challenged students to accept Rachel's challenge to adopt kindness and compassion for their schools. After it was all over, our student presenters were exhausted. Some of them had done as many as four assemblies in one day. And those who were involved behind the scenes were equally exhausted. But the week demonstrated that Rachel's little essay had now started a chain reaction in the lives of those in El Paso, Texas.

We still get hundreds of e-mails every week from students in El Paso telling us stories of how their schools have changed. People are a little kinder in many of the schools. Classes periodically still take time to talk about Rachel and how her Codes of Life can make a difference in their lives.

Here are just two of the many e-mails we have received from young people who experienced Rachel's Challenge in El Paso.

Hi, I'm a student at J.M. Hanks High School in El Paso, Texas. Today was a very important day for me. I had the most fortunate opportunity to listen to the story of a young girl, and her friends and family that were affected by her tragedy. I would like to say thank you so much from the bottom of my heart for coming to visit us.

Our presentation was so heartfelt and moving, and I was sitting there thinking, "I wish I could do something for them." Then I realized that I could. What you came to my school to do was to get the message across that even the smallest smile can make a difference. By remembering Rachel's theory and beliefs, she will live on, and the world will become a better place.

That is my gift to you. I wanted to write you all because I greatly respect what you're doing. I know this is probably another letter to add to your stacks of letters, but your presentation today (I saw it twice) really changed my life.

A couple days ago, I had cut off my best friends because I felt I wasn't fitting in with them, and it was over a stupid argument. I felt that everyone in the world was against me. This afternoon, I walked up to my friend, and gave her a hug.

Today you taught forgiveness. My friend and I didn't even have to exchange words; we both understood each other, and now, I have a loving friend to walk the halls with.

Losing Rachel, no doubt, must have been the most terrible event in your entire life, but I truly believe that God works in mysterious ways and that this is all part of a greater plan. You wouldn't be talking to schools like mine if it hadn't happened and what you did today, boys, was the most honorable experience I've ever had. I've had opportunities to meet extremely important people in our nation before, but none influenced me as much as you did. Please be strong and know that while you're in Colorado, a girl in El Paso, Texas has grieved for your sister and your loss, but keeps Rachel's memory strong. I know this will be something I'll pass on to my children.

From El Paso to the Nation

After our success in El Paso, we have expanded the Rachel's Challenge program, which now features the assembly program for all students, a two-hour training session for dedicated students who really want to invest time and effort in making their schools better places, and a one-hour session for teachers and parents.

Along the way, talented new individuals have joined our team. Danny Orr has been a special gift of God to this work. Danny was a professional baseball player before a career-ending injury. I met Danny while he was a Fellowship of Christian Athletes director in Wyoming. Danny had invited me to come and speak to several thousand students and parents in Jackson Hole and Rock Springs, Wyoming. On the long drive between those two cities my wife, Sandy, Danny, and I began to talk about some of the spiritual influences in Rachel's life. Danny began to weep as we talked about these things, and at one point had to pull the car over to the side of the road.

On that trip the Lord really put a bond between Danny and us. So much so that he and his wife, Jodi, and their three children now reside in

Phoenix, Arizona, where Danny directs the Rachel's Challenge program.

As our team was completing the resource manual for the training sessions, I experienced another of many divine appointments, meeting Gene Bedley, a former national Teacher of the Year and director of a wonderful organization called Character Counts. Gene offered to help us put the final touches on our material and help publicize Rachel's Challenge to five thousand schools that have incorporated Character Counts into their curriculum. Our program has now been conducted in hundreds of schools across America, and it is always a delight to read the stories from students, parents, and teachers following a day at their school.

We have been privileged to take Rachel's code of ethics to young people across the country, and they have responded with a flood of e-mails. Here are just a few of the e-mails they have sent us.

From a high school student in Washington:

When I first heard there was to be an assembly on Monday, I was not as excited as I normally was. I didn't realize the impact it was going to make on me. I sat watching in stunned silence.

Rachel was a great student. I never knew her, but I know that if I could meet her, I would fall in love with her personality and character. I feel I have missed out because of not knowing her. I think about her and become teary-eyed, but I know that this will make a difference. I printed a photo of Rachel and placed it carefully in my binder with her "My Ethics, My Codes of Life" report. Rachel and her life inspire me to become a better person.

The impact of the assembly was great, not just on me. That day, the students in my school were much kinder. People went out of their way to do something good for their friends. Hugs were given to every student. I hope it stays this way, however I do not believe it will, but I will always remember, I will not forget what happened. Thank you so much.

From a middle school student in Illinois:

I really enjoyed your coming. It inspired me to reach out to other kids that are different than me. I realized everything is not about me and how I feel, but about how others feel and respond to other kids' comments.

After the assembly I evaluated how I am living my life and how I can change. It doesn't matter if you are popular or not; it matters who you are inside. Thanks for helping me realize what I can do differently in my life.

From a high school student in Pennsylvania:

To me, the essay that Rachel wrote was very touching and had a lot of meaning. It opened my eyes and I'm sure a lot of other people's eyes too. She looked beneath the surface of a misfit, lonely person and saw the good in him/her and did her best to encourage them. Not a lot of people have the guts to do that, and I admire the people who do. Because they are only trying to make the world a better place to live in. And there are only so many of them in the world. So I think that we all need to reach out to someone. You may prevent a terrible tragedy. It's not too much to ask to hold a door open or say hi; how can you ever regret it? Remember, "You may just start a chain reaction." Thanks.

This was from a high school student in Iowa who heard a presentation by Barry and Sue Kraft, who head up our Rachel's Challenge office in Colorado:

I would just like you to know that after Barry talked to us you could just feel a change in our school. It was a great feeling knowing that just one person could do that and I was amazed that he had such an impact on our school with his story on Rachel. I just can't explain it with words.

I would also like you to know that after the session with Barry and his wife, Sue, I have started to change my life. I went up to a girl that I just couldn't stand and told her I was sorry for being so rude to her behind her back and to her face. Do you know what she said . . . that she forgave me and then she hugged me. And yet I have no idea why someone would do that to me after the way I was. It was just amazing.

The best feeling was knowing that I was changing. It was awesome and I wanted to thank Barry and Sue for their trust in me. I don't think I could have done it without them and our Lord and Savior JESUS CHRIST. He is an awesome person and I can just see him and Rachel looking down on Barry and Sue. Once again I thank you from the bottom of my heart.

And this e-mail came from a junior high student in Iowa:

Hi. You came to our high school today and that assembly you put on touched my heart in many ways I can't begin to explain how much I loved that. You definitely kept your promise . . . I think (in my opinion) the whole assembly touched me the most. I realized that all people need is kindness and bullying shouldn't go on. I know you told us that everyone replies back to you and says they want to change or make a difference . . . or something along the lines of that . . . well it's true because I want to too.

That was the BEST assembly I've had my whole life. I've decided to totally change after hearing Rachel's story. I realized her personality is the kind that will get you a lot of friends and you will be like[d] by everyone . . . well I've decided that I have a new role model. When you were talking about how you would be here for anyone and stuff . . . I just started crying . . . that was the sweetest thing I've heard in a while. I want that attitude too and I think if you just believe in yourself anything can happen. I will also live today like there will not be a tomorrow.

Thanks sooo much for visiting our school. . .it was totally worth our time! Hope to hear from you soon.

Reading, Writing, and Revenge

Columbine wasn't the first school to experience shootings and death, and sadly it wasn't the last. Enraged students have been turning classrooms into sites of carnage for more than two decades. As we think about some of these terrible attacks, it becomes increasingly clear to me that we desperately need programs like Rachel's Challenge to help turn the tide.

It's encouraging to know that in the wake of Columbine, greater attentiveness by students, school officials, and law enforcement personnel has actually helped thwart an estimated sixty planned attacks across the country, in places like Cupertino, California; Elmira, New York; New Bedford, Massachusetts; Fort Collins, Colorado; and Hoyt, Kansas.

Now that people know what kinds of evil and violence are possible, more of them are on the lookout for signs of trouble.

Try a Little Tenderness

Of course, as hundreds of students from across America have told me over the years, a shooting doesn't have to take place to make school a living hell for some of its students. When she was alive, Rachel's heart went out to students who were alienated outsiders because they were continually harassed and bullied by others, making their school years a time of torment.

In the schools where our Rachel's Challenge team has conducted assemblies or other activities, both bullies and those who have bullied have responded to Rachel's message of love and compassion. Some of the e-mails we have received testify to the impact these events have had.

> I was very touched by how Rachel made that boy Adam feel special and didn't pick on him like the rest did for his problem. I was one that cared about people and some of my friends in fifth grade thought it was wrong for me to care about a boy who had cancer and looked different from the rest of us. I told him that no matter what people say[,] you have the greatest gift ever, and that you are no different from everyone else and you're a lot stronger in your heart and to never let people take you down. After I said that to him it was for a moment that he actually realized he had a friend. Three months after that he died.

> Rachel did an extraordinary thing for people. She will always be remembered for that. If I had to leave the world today, I would not be satisfied with who I have become and how I have acted towards others in my student body.

> The speaker I heard made me realize what it feels like to be picked on and made fun of. When I was in elementary and middle school, people made fun of me right and left because I had a speech impediment. They also made fun of me for other reasons and a few times I've felt I'd hit my last resort. So when I stood up to say I'll take Rachel's Challenge, I meant it. Meaning I'm

going to stand up for the kids who get picked on and not pick on anyone and treat everyone with the same respect.

Just like any other school, we have our groups and cliques. I have to admit that I too have separated myself from other people because they are not like me. I used to be more nice, but it seems as though one of my friends is keeping me from talking to people unlike us. I'd like to put myself up to Rachel's Challenge, but I do NOT want to lose my best friend.

I have to admit I used to be one of the people that got picked on. Then I changed into the person that picks on people. Now that I see what happens I decided to not ever pick on people again, at least I'll try because I would never want to hurt any of my classmates. I'm going to try to be more like Rachel.

I am one of those kids who are in between gang and just friends and now I think I have gotten some new information and I want to do everything in my power to spread the word about Rachel Scott. This assembly brought me to tears.

I went out of my way to take on that challenge. I asked a not so cool girl to sit by me in Social Studies. She said yes and I saw the first smile in a long time come across her face. And the boys in my class started laughing because I was hanging out with her, but I just looked at her and thought, "You know I should be the one laughing cause I am doing so much more than they can imagine. I am taking on Rachel's challenge and reaching out to others."

I am one that some people would call a bully some of the times. I felt really moved by the speaker. After I got back to school I was nice to everybody and said hi to everybody I saw. So [from] now on I am going to try to be nice to everybody.

I read the book, *Rachel's Tears*, during my junior year of high school. After reading about the relationship she had with God, I realized that I wanted that too. I wanted to reach out to the outcasts of my school. I wanted to take a stand. I vowed that I would carry Rachel's torch. I started to see people differently. Before I read the book I overlooked so many people. I was quick to judge others, not trying to understand who these people were. What their lives were like. What their dreams were. What they loved. I would carry the book to my classes and other people would see it sitting on my desk and ask what it was about. I would tell them and they'd ask if they could borrow it. I had so many people wanting to borrow it that I had to make a list to keep track.

How is it possible that an hour long talk by a total stranger can so radically change someone's life? But that is exactly what happened to me. I was a totally different person before. I thought it was cool to hang out with the popular crowd and make fun of kids who weren't so cool. But now, after hearing about how Rachel lived her life, I want to do everything within my power to reach out to the "unreached." I am now helping kids with problems and talking with kids that don't have friends. I never realized how fulfilling it can be to really li[v]e your life to help others!

Barry tells about an incident that happened at one of the schools where he was talking to students:

During an assembly I was explaining how easy it is to pick on people who are weak. I asked the audience a rhetorical question: "Why is it that we pick on those who aren't able to defend themselves?"

A hand went up immediately in the back row. The student stood up, and with a slight slur in his speech, addressed his classmates.

"I am a little slower than most of you and I am different, but I want you all to know that it hurts when you pick on me. Just because I act like it doesn't bother me and I try to be cool about it, I want you to know it hurts me."

The students were quiet except for a clean-cut kid near the front who began to cry. When the presentation was over, the slow student, wearing baggy pants and gold chains, walked down to the front to shake my hand. The clean-cut kid who'd been crying came down and took a front seat on the bleachers. When all the students and teachers who wanted to talk to me left, this clean-cut kid came up and hugged me. He said he was one of those who had picked on the slower student. He was crushed by the fact that he'd never thought about anyone else's feelings.

He assured me that from that day forward he would be nice to everyone. Another life changed by Rachel.

A Movement Continues

These are just a few of the thousands of e-mails that students have sent us or posted on our Web site (www.rachelschallenge.com).

We love hearing from people, but we're not stopping now. We know so many more young people need to hear Rachel's message, so we have continued to expand our programs and team of speakers. We have also added a national director and a growing number of regional representatives. I think Rachel would smile at the incredible impact her little two-page report has had on thousands of people in the last year. But it's just the beginning.

Rachel's Challenge is destined to be implemented in schools across the country as this book is being written. I dare to think, as she challenged us to do, what a difference the kindness and compassion that started in a high school essay will make.

(If you want to take up Rachel's Challenge in a school in your community, please contact the Rachel's Challenge office at 303-346-1300 or send us a message on our Web site, www.rachelschallenge.com).

Five

Picking Up the Torch

Rachel's funeral was held on the Saturday after the Columbine killings. Those who sat in the packed church heard Pastor Bruce Porter issue a powerful challenge, a challenge that was heard by millions more people who watched the funeral as it was broadcast live on CNN.

Here's what Pastor Porter said:

> Young people here today, hear me. I want to issue a challenge to each and every one of you. Don't despair of life, don't despair of what has happened to you.

Rachel carried a torch, the torch of truth, the torch of compassion, a torch of love, the torch of the good news of Jesus Christ, her Savior and Lord, who she was not ashamed of even in her hour of death.

I want to lay a challenge before each and every one of you young people here today. The torch has fallen from Rachel's hand. Who will pick it up again? Who will pick up the torch again?

One of the most thrilling things I have experienced during the past three years is to witness people of all ages and from all parts of the country doing what they can to pick up Rachel's torch and make a positive difference in the world.

In this chapter, I want to tell the stories of a few of these torchbearers. In addition, I want to describe some of the good things that have been inspired by two other committed Christians who were killed at Columbine. It is my hope that the stories in this chapter will both comfort and encourage those who have been touched by Columbine and by Rachel's message. Beyond that, these stories show that people of faith and hope can see the outlines of God's infinite blessings in even the most tragic circumstances of life.

A Sister's Service

Rachel was close to her two brothers and two sisters and was dearly loved by them all. But during the last two years of her life, she probably spent more time with Dana than any other member of the family. Rachel and Dana attended the same youth group at Orchard Road Christian Center, and went there together several times a week for various activities.

Anyone who knows Dana will tell you that she is the shyest, quietest member of our family. She has a dignified grace about her that I have always admired, but of all my children, Dana was the least likely to become a public speaker. So guess who became the spokesperson of the family from among Rachel's siblings? You guessed it! Quiet, shy Dana.

Our family is so proud of the way she has presented Rachel's story to hundreds of thousands of young people in the three years since Rachel died. At the time I was writing this book, Dana had already spoken in more than 125 high school and middle school assemblies in 36 states and had shared Rachel's story more than 175 times in churches, conferences, camps, workshops, and youth rallies. These numbers will grow even larger by the time you read these words.

Although Dana isn't flamboyant or flashy, she has a passion for talking about Rachel's message, and that passion is conveyed every time she speaks.

Dana speaking with students

Here's what Susan Narveson, a reporter for a newspaper in Bagley, Minnesota, had to say about a presentation Dana gave there in April 2002:

Dana said, "Even though I lost my sister and could've easily lost my brother and two cousins, I want to share from my heart some really good things that have come from the tragedy."

Dana told students that she wanted her presentation to "give more courage, hope in your life, but also a challenge what you can do in your school.

"Our generation has had two defining moments. It began with Columbine and then 9/11. Our priorities have changed, people have become real important again. I had a choice after Rachel died. I could be an angry and bitter person or a better person.

"I'm not going to lie to you—if you choose to reach out to someone, it might cost you. It takes a real person of moral strength and conviction—it is a road less traveled."

Several graduates from the 1970s were brought back to thoughts of a classmate who was bullied and teased unmercifully, and who eventually ended his own life.

One student said, "While that tragedy at least momentarily brought students to their knees in grief and drew people together, I still wonder if it could have been avoided altogether, had people been kind.

One senior girl said of her impression of Dana: "Just looking at her in her jeans and hoodie—she looked so small and alone sitting in that blue folding chair, but she had a big message. It made me almost feel like Rachel was my sister too."

We Are Weak but God Is Strong

Dana will be the first to tell you that God has taken her greatest area of weakness (public speaking) and allowed His strength to be made evident through her. I believe many of the other people who have picked up Rachel's torch have also experienced the same sense of divine empowerment.

The story of Dana's public ministry really began when Rachel performed a mime to the Ray Boltz song "Watch the Lamb" at a Columbine talent show a little more than a year before her death. Dana was so impressed with the performance that she asked Rachel to teach it to her so that she could do it at her youth group. Rachel promised that she would, but days turned into weeks and Dana had still not been taught the mime. Every few months Dana would remind Rachel that she wanted to learn it and Rachel would agree to teach it to her and then promptly forget her promise.

This pattern of reminding and forgetting continued for more than a year, until one night, a week before Rachel was killed, she turned to Dana and said, "Dana, it's time for you to learn 'Watch the Lamb'!" Dana says she will never forget those several hours as she and her sister practiced the mime in the basement until Dana had memorized it. And no one knew it at the time, but Rachel began the process of passing the torch to Dana that night. Neither of them knew that Dana would be performing "Watch the Lamb" in Rachel's memory thousands of times in the years ahead.

Exactly one year and one week later, Dana would perform the mime before the world at an internationally televised event commemorating the first anniversary of the Columbine tragedy. As Dana performed the mime on stage, the large projection screen behind her lit up with a video clip of Rachel performing the same movements. The video was taken at the high school talent show where Rachel first performed it herself. I sat on the platform at the memorial event watching Dana perform the mime, and I wept as I watched my two daughters portraying the story of Calvary for the eyes of the world.

Dana performs at the one-year anniversary of the Columbine tragedy

Sitting with me on that platform were two men who participated in the memorial—Christian speaker Josh McDowell and Colorado Governor Bill Owens. In his comment that day, Governor Owens spoke for many of us in the audience. "Today is about the angels who are watching over us—helping us to heal and helping us to remember," he told the crowd gathered at the state capitol in Denver. He then presided over a moment of silence that marked the precise instant Dylan Klebold and Eric Harris began killing twelve students and a teacher and wounding another twenty-six people. In addition, thirteen balloons lifted off into the air as a bell tolled thirteen times.

"Too often over the last year, the coverage of the tragedy at Columbine High School has focused on the two young men who so viciously took the lives of our loved ones and friends," said Governor Owens, "but not today." The truth of these words has been proven hundreds of times since then, as Dana does her part to bring redemption out of tragedy.

A Reluctant Celebrity

Dana and I occasionally get the chance to minister together at large youth events where I speak and she performs "Watch the Lamb." It never fails to bring tears to the eyes of the audience members, who often rise to their feet to give her a standing ovation.

Dana told me once that she sometimes feels as though she just moves aside during the performance and allows the memory of Rachel to minister to the crowd. She also said that she receives the applause and appreciation and simply lifts it up to heaven, believing that God will place the accolades at Rachel's feet.

There have been weeks when Dana has had a brutal schedule, doing as many as five events in one day (four school assemblies and an evening event). Yet I have never heard her complain. She simply smiles and moves on to the next event. Dana has taught me things that she'll never realize. She is one of my heroes.

And her work has been getting attention. Here's part of an article about one of Dana's presentations, written by Elizabeth Coyle, a staff writer for the *Bedford Gazette* in Bedford, Pennsylvania:

Rachel's older sister, Dana, told students at Bedford High School Wednesday that she is a messenger for her late sister, who thought that if she could show one person an act of kindness, it might spread to others.

Dana is touring the country, telling high school students about her sister's life and her desire for everyone to follow Rachel's example.

Rachel's Challenge, as she calls it, asks school students to begin to show more compassion to fellow students.

"Our society doesn't teach us to take care of one another. We're basically being given the message to look out for yourself," Dana said.

In reading from her sister's diaries, "I got to see the depth and complexity of her," Dana said.

Rachel wrote that she decided to reach out to three groups of people at the school: new people, those with handicaps and those who were picked on, Dana said.

In a sprawling campus of 1,800 students, school life could be tough on a student, Dana said. "The school had a reputation for being stuck-up and cliquish," Dana said.

Speaking about how Rachel was kind to Adam, a student with a muscular disease, Dana said, "Rachel said that you never know how far a little kindness can go. She had no idea that random kindness went so far."

Dana doesn't speak harshly of the two boys who were responsible for the shooting, the pipe bombs and the destruction. "The two gunmen needed friends just as much as anyone else," Dana said. "One person could have made a difference in their lives."

Dana Strikes a Chord

I am moved by Dana's presentations, but then again, I am her father. But apparently I am not the only person who has received encouragement and inspiration from her ministry.

We heard from a dairy farmer in Pennsylvania who owned a herd of several hundred cows that kept him busy from dawn until dusk seven days a week. This man's son heard Rachel's story at a high school assembly and bought a copy of the book *Rachel's Journals*. The son took the book home that night and his dad happened to see it. After several days the farmer picked it up one evening and began reading it. He was so touched by Rachel's writing that he immediately bought a copy of *Rachel's Tears*.

Rachel's story struck this man's heart and emotions at a deep level. He suddenly began to realize that he was spending all of his time with cows instead of his family! He wept as he read, and a sense of direction began to emerge. He decided to sell his farm so he would have more time to spend with his family.

Roughly a year after that transition, he raised the funds to have Dana come back to his area of Pennsylvania to speak in schools and at a community outreach event. This dear brother has become a faithful supporter of our work, both in prayer and finances of the Columbine Redemption, our nonprofit organization.

"Rachel has inspired me to 'walk my talk' and given me an urgency to witness to others," he said. "God has used your beloved Rachel to help a total stranger get his focus on eternal things again."

Once again a chain reaction had started. God used Rachel's story to impact a farmer's entire family, right down to the cows, who have a new owner!

Dana hasn't yet traveled to other countries to share Rachel's story, but she did have the chance to talk by telephone with eight hundred young people in Sweden! People organizing a Swedish youth gathering asked Dana to give her presentation to the group via telephone. Dana listened on the phone as hundreds of Swedish young people sang and worshiped together. Then the crowd grew quiet, and for the next forty-five minutes, Dana challenged the young people with her sister's testimony. A translator presented her words in Swedish.

"Dad, it was so beautiful to hear hundreds of young people applauding, whistling, and expressing their thanks to me for sharing Rachel's story with them," she said.

So thanks to God and the wonders of modern technology, Rachel's story has gone out to places none of us have even visited.

Taking the Message to America's Schools

In another chapter of this book we talk about the Rachel's Challenge school program. Thanks to the help of many people, including school administrators in many parts of the country, we have been able to take Rachel's message to some of the people who need to hear it most—young people who attend America's schools.

There are a number of speakers who work with us, going into high schools and middle schools with a program about Rachel's message of caring and compassion. But our primary speaker from the beginning has been Dana. We consistently hear from principals, teachers, and students that it is the most powerful assembly they have ever attended. Here are examples of the numerous e-mails that flood our office:

I was at school today and heard a girl named Dana talk about her sister Rachel who had been shot and killed at her school. Rachel wrote about starting a chain reaction of kindness and I cried as I watched the video about her life and how she wanted to change the world. I have decided that I will be a part of her chain reaction and will start being kind to others.

I have treated people bad at my school sometimes. I am in the 8th grade and I just wanted Dana to know that I was paying attention to what she said and I cried. Her speech made me think about my life and how I would like to be like her sister and do good things. I came home from school and cleaned my room. My mom asked me what had caused me to do that and I told her about Dana and her sister, Rachel.

This e-mail came from a teacher in Florida:

Dear Scott Family:
I was utterly amazed when I heard Dana speak at our school today. As she spoke about your family forgiving the families of the boys who committed those horrible actions at Columbine, I was deeply convicted of my own anger at my ex-husband.

I realized as Dana spoke, that I had allowed my life to be consumed with bitterness and anger about something that I was helpless to change. I sat there and listened to Dana and I thought, "If she can forgive the ones who killed her own dear sister, then I can forgive and let go of the rage built up inside of me!"

I thought I was attending that assembly to give support to my students, but believe me, that assembly was for me.

Over the next few days I wept buckets of tears and just felt totally cleansed from all my bitterness. I have made a decision to refuse to be controlled by things I can't change. I will not be an unforgiving, hard, callused person!

Thank you, Dana, for starting a chain reaction in me.

Dana speaking at an assembly

Another middle schooler sent this e-mail to Dana:

I'm so glad you came to my school. You inspired me to reach out to other kids that are different from me. I now realize that everything is not just about me and how I feel, but about how others feel also. It doesn't matter whether you are popular or not—it matters who you are inside.

Thanks you so much for helping me see that I can make a difference.

Hope Survives Death

I have also been amazed to see how two other committed Christian young people who were killed at Columbine have also left a legacy of hope that has transformed people's lives. Stories like these show that the ground swell movement that has emerged from the chaos of Columbine is much larger than Rachel.

John Tomlin was a wonderful young man who was murdered in the library at Columbine on that day in April 1999. John had spent part of the previous summer traveling to Mexico, where he helped build homes for the homeless and participated in missions activities. Over the past three years, John's parents, John and Doreen Tomlin, have been a source of love and encouragement for me and my wife, Sandy. They have told us some unique stories about their son.

Darrell (center) with John and Doreen Tomlin

Several months before he was murdered, John's mom asked him the oddest question. "John, if anything ever were to happen to you, where would you want to be buried?" John looked at her and said, "Mom, I want to be buried in Wisconsin, because my best friend lives there." To this day, Doreen doesn't know why she even brought up this subject with him, but later she would be glad she had.

The night before John died, two other unusual things happened. First, John's younger sister Ashley went downstairs to give John a goodnight hug. She made a habit of doing that every night before she went to bed. She loved and looked up to her older brother.

However, this night something was different. As she walked into the room, she had a feeling that she would never get to see John alive again. She felt so strongly about it that she hugged him extra long that night.

The next morning she jumped out of bed in time to look out the window and see John getting into his pickup truck to head for Columbine. She remembers thinking, "See, Ashley, it was just a dream. You got to see John again!" Little did she realize that it would be the last memory she would have of John before he was murdered.

The night before his death, John stayed up until after 2 A.M. talking on the phone with his girlfriend, Michelle Oetter. She was sharing with John about some problems she was having with one of her friends. As their conversation wound down and they were close to saying good-bye, Michelle recalls that John said the strangest thing. He said, "Michelle, I know you're going through some tough times in your relationship with your friend, but even if I'm not around to help, remember that you can always turn to God."

Michelle believes that John had a sense, like Rachel did, that something was about to happen. His final words will forever echo in her mind.

A Girlfriend Remembers

Michelle wrote about her memories of John in *Rachel's Journal*, a magazine that was published by The Columbine Redemption. One of her memories concerned one of her early dates with John.

I was floored by what a gentleman he was. We pulled into the parking lot at the movie theater and both got out of the truck. John stopped and looked at me across the hood. I turned to see what he was waiting on and he asked me what I was doing.

I gave him a very confused look and asked if we were still going to see the movie. He said, "Yes," and then asked me why I had gotten out of the truck.

Then, with the most honest and sincere look in his eyes, he said, "Michelle, I don't know about other guys you have gone out with, but as long as you are with me you will never, ever touch a door."

As I stood there speechless, I realized that John Tomlin was nothing like any guy I had ever known."

Another date with John was equally memorable:

He took me to Red Lobster for Valentine's Day. I know that might not seem like a big deal, but as we were getting ready to order, he looked up and told me he didn't know what to get, that he really didn't like fish.

I asked him why we were at Red Lobster if he didn't like fish and he told me that he had heard me tell a friend once how much I loved it.

He was the answer to prayer that showed me real love isn't words, it isn't kisses, and it isn't empty promises. John showed me that real love is wanting to be with someone exactly for who they are, and being able to sacrifice some things to be together.

In the wake of John's death, Michelle saw a number of his friends remember his commitment to Christ.

On the Wednesday night after the shooting, I asked John's best friend if he would come to youth group with me. I knew he wasn't a Christian, and John and I had been praying for him since we had started dating. John had asked him to come to church every week, and there was always a different reason why he couldn't make it. That night he came, and as we sat in the youth room and prayed together and cried together and told stories of John, the friend began to understand that there was something missing. Later that night he accepted Christ as his personal Savior.

This was an answer to John's prayers.

A Memory Living On

Michelle and everyone else who knew John knew he loved driving his big Chevrolet pickup truck through mud and snow. John had just gotten his driver's license before his death and had bought his dream truck with money he had been saving since he was fourteen.

That truck, which like Rachel's car was parked in the Columbine school lot on the day of the shootings, became a sort of memorial in the parking lot. John was buried in Wisconsin in a satin-lined coffin embroidered with Chevy trucks.

Later, a Chevrolet employee became aware of John's affection for the company's trucks after seeing John's parents on *Oprah*. In 2001, Chevrolet, along with Habitat for Humanity and members of the Tomlin family and other families, built a house in Lakewood, Colorado.

Today the "John Tomlin Memorial House" provides a home for a family that previously didn't have a place to stay. A plaque on the outside of the house features Psalm 27:1: "The LORD is my light and my salvation—whom shall I fear?"

John's story reminds me of an episode from the life of Jesus.

Jesus understood both the purpose and the pain that was intended for His life. After three and a half years of ministry, He told His disciples that His time had come. They thought He was going to take over Rome and establish an earthly kingdom, but He was speaking of His death and of establishing a spiritual kingdom. His final words reflected the completeness of His mission on earth: "It is finished" (John 19:30).

The apostle Paul was a man who faced death many times. He was shipwrecked, beaten on several occasions, and even left for dead a time or two. But Paul kept the faith until it became clear he would face death for his service to Christ. It was then that Paul wrote these immortal words: "The time of my departure is at hand. I have fought a good fight, I have finished my course, I have kept the faith" (2 Tim. 4:7 KJV).

I am sure John Tomlin would agree.

The Girl Who Said Yes

Days after the Columbine killings, *The Washington Post* reported on the motives of the two troubled killers: "There is no evidence that the murderous pair moved through the corridors with a hit list of names. But it was widely known among Columbine students that the tiny subculture to which Harris and Klebold belonged had little tolerance for devout Christians," said the article.

In the following days and weeks, a devout Christian named Cassie Bernall became one of the most visible symbols of the Columbine tragedy. In a book entitled *She Said Yes*, Cassie's mother told the story of Cassie's years of rebellion, her eventual conversion to faith in Christ, and her boldness in speaking out for Christ at Columbine. That boldness may have contributed to her death.

But as with John Tomlin, Cassie's impact didn't end with her death.

Maria Moore, a doctor from Hendersonville, North Carolina, and her husband, Mark, an emergency medicine physician, were moved by the Columbine tragedy. "I was really very touched by Cassie's story; how she believed in God and how she lost her life," said Dr. Moore. "I felt that God wanted me to support a ministry that came out of this."

Inspired by Cassie, the Moores helped raise $300,000 to build an orphanage in the Latin American country of Honduras. Today, the orphanage cares for abandoned children and is operated by the Christian Mission of Central Honduras, a nondenominational organization based in Hendersonville.

In April 2001, James B. Meadow, a staff writer with Denver's *Rocky Mountain News*, visited the orphanage and wrote the following words:

Here, 3,100 miles from the dry plains of Colorado, where the bark of the Indio Desnudo tree is so silvery it is incandescent and the singing of neon-bright birds explodes at sunrise into an exotic glee club, where the land is lush and rich but the people are wretchedly poor, here, the blood of Cassie Bernall is nourishing a legacy of hope and salvation for the kind of children she would have loved.

Out of the ashes and carnage that was Columbine has risen in this place a better future—the Hogar de Niños Cassie Rene Bernall, a home for children; a day-care ministry and a soon-to-be orphanage in the backwater heartland of one of Latin America's poorest countries.

It is a cheerful yellow-and-white two-story building, a structure built to withstand earthquakes and nurture the needy; both a symbol and a reality that came about thanks to the generosity of two people and the sweat of many others—none of whom had ever heard of Bernall, 17, until her life was tragically ended.

How a blond teenager from the American suburbs became the catalyst for desperately needed services for black-haired, brown-eyed Third World children is a unique story of love and faith transcending geographic and cultural differences."

As Dr. Moore told the reporter, "If there had been no Columbine, there would not have been an orphanage."

Beauty in God's Service

In 1999, I spoke in Michigan, where I met a beautiful young woman named Rachel Wandell. Rachel told me that she had been inspired by Rachel Scott and wanted to start some activities in her community.

I didn't hear anything for a while, then Rachel wrote the following letter, which was published in *Rachel's Journal* magazine:

I'm the one who told you that I wanted to start a Bible study in my school and dedicate it in honor of your amazing daughter. It's called J.O.Y. Ministries (Jesus & Our Youth).

It's not only a simple Bible study for Christians and their comfort zone, but it will reach out to those who don't know God but want to do something incredible in their community. This ministry will be founded on random acts of kindness, just as your Rachel portrayed in her life.

I have already talked to my superintendent and he has agreed to support this ministry and let me use the school facility to hold the meetings. Since this ministry will be founded in your daughter's memory, I feel that the best way to open it up is to retell the Columbine story and Rachel's life and how it has been a spiritual event.

Soon after this we received a follow-up from Rachel:

We have 20-30 people each week and one teacher! At least 10 have accepted Christ for the first time. We do community service projects each month, and today was our first. We raked leaves for a predominantly elderly community and received a $40 donation blessing that we will use on the 30th of October. On that date we are going to Hospice of Lenawee County and painting pumpkins with the terminally ill children. We are also starting a J.O.Y. Ministries web site.

The next time we heard from Rachel, she had won a regional Michigan beauty pageant and was competing for the honor of Miss Michigan 2001. Although she didn't win the top prize, she did finish in the top ten.

Rachel says some of the public speaking she had been doing about Columbine helped her in the poise and presentation categories. As she explained to a local reporter: "I'm not someone who gets nervous. I've spoken for over 30 churches and organizations, so I'm used to it." Her speaking has been on behalf of an effort she launched called Commitment to Kindness. Rachel started the program in her high school and used it as her community service project in the pageant.

The main feature of Commitment to Kindness is Bible studies that incorporate random acts of kindness in the local community. For Rachel, a central part of her work is to prevent future Columbines. "I focus on bullying and teasing," she says. "Two-thirds of recent school shootings involved bullying and teasing. So out of the 235 who have died, 156 were caused by people who were teased and couldn't get over it."

For her talent portion of the Miss Michigan pageant, Rachel performed a mime to the "Watch the Lamb" song. "I don't sing," she says. "I don't dance. I don't twirl the baton. I don't have any of the stereotypical talents of beauty pageant contestants."

But Rachel does have a burning desire to spread a message of commitment and concern that was sparked by another young woman named Rachel. "Rachel Scott didn't hold back her compassion, and I realized I sometimes do."

I am deeply gratified by people like Rachel Wandell, who use their God-given talents to promote a message of hope and healing. There are so many additional exciting stores I could share if this book a few hundred more pages, but I think you get the idea.

God doesn't expect you to be a perfect speaker, a wonderful singer, or even Miss Michigan to serve Him. All it takes is love for Him, love for people, and a willingness to go wherever God sends you and do what He wants you to do.

Are you willing to pick up the torch and follow these examples? If so, you too can make a positive difference in our world.

Six

More Than Kid Stuff

It has been exciting to see thousands of young people work to transform their schools from places of fear and intimidation into places where Rachel's values of compassion and caring now have powerful impact. Perhaps even more amazing has been the fact that many adults have told me that Rachel's story has had a life-changing influence in their lives and the lives of others they know.

In our culture today, young people and adults often look at each other, if at all, across a yawning generational divide. But the tragedy of Columbine was an event that pulled young and old together. And now, three years later, adults continue to be touched and transformed by the life of one young woman who dared to trust God and reach out to others in His name.

One e-mail came from an emergency room nurse:

Today while at work, I was trying to finish reading your book, *Rachel's Tears*, during a slow time. I put the book down for a few minutes, and another employee picked it up and before she even realized it she had read 25 pages. She isn't a Christian and has had several bad encounters with overzealous Christians who have attempted to "push the gospel" on her. I have secretly prayed for her for a long time, and I can see that Rachel's story is at work in her heart. I had to send you this e-mail just to let you know how Rachel reaches people in the most unexpected ways.

Another came from a police chief who had met me during a speaking engagement:

I met you and gave you a ride to the Victim's Rights Conference in Atlantic City, NJ. Your presentation of your daughter's life was so powerful and moving that I haven't stopped thinking about Rachel since that time. She must have been an angel sent from God to try and make a difference with our youth. I have been in law enforcement for 33 years and will soon be retiring, but before I do I want to carry Rachel's message to as many students as possible. Thank you for your inspiration.

A thirty-eight-year-old businessman from California had this to say: "I can't ever understand the pain you've gone through. I look at my baby girl and I can't begin to process it. Columbine was a major turning point in the war between good and evil. I'll never be the same. I'm eternally grateful for your daughter's gift to us." And even a Marine from Panama City, Florida, told us he had drawn courage from Rachel's example: "I'm in the

Marine Corps, and I have learned to use courage, honor, and commitment to defeat the enemy. But I think that Rachel is the true meaning of honor, courage, and commitment to Jesus Christ."

It has been especially gratifying to see Christians from all kinds of denominational backgrounds and traditions find God's truth in portions of Rachel's story. One day I received a letter from a Greek Orthodox banker from Montclair, New Jersey, who had just written a book of his own and was writing to request permission to dedicate his book to Rachel:

> It is not without a bit of trepidation that we write to you and your family, to request your permission to remember your daughter, Rachel, in the dedication of a Christian book we hope to have published soon. We did not know your daughter, but at the same time, as Christians we do know something about a heart full of faith in our Lord Jesus Christ, and your daughter's incredible and heroic martyrdom speaks in a way that no words would ever say.

Of course, we gladly granted his request.

And in other cases, Columbine has given people renewed confidence to pursue the callings they believe they have received from God. A twenty-five-year-old woman from Wilkes-Barre, Pennsylvania, wrote us this encouraging letter: "I am 25 years old and working towards my Master's degree in Elementary School Counseling. Up until the night I met you, I was having doubts about whether or not I was entering into the right career field. You said many powerful things that evening and now I know that I AM in the right field."

A Journey Toward Faith and Service

Donald K. Lewis, who is forty-six years old, is the executive director of the Moon Area Support Organization and the Care for Youth Initiative in Pittsburgh, Pennsylvania.

Before Columbine, Don was focused primarily on his own success and happiness, but now he is working to help young people in Moon Township, a suburb located twenty minutes west of downtown Pittsburgh. His organization's mission is to recruit servant leaders in the area who can have a positive influence on youth struggling with sexual issues, drug and alcohol abuse, domestic violence, eating disorders, depression, and Internet stalking. The organization provides mentoring and is affiliated with organizations that can provide professional help and facilitation services to help both the youth and their families.

We asked Don to write about his experience, and he gladly did so.

Around January 1999, I began to question the purpose of life. I was struggling both in my career and personal life. Outwardly, I was experiencing outstanding success in my career, held multiple advanced degrees from various universities, married an incredible woman named Karen, and we were blessed with a wonderful daughter named Michelle.

I had obtained material and financial wealth and continued to be blessed with great family and friends. However, it seemed like my life was passing before me in an instant.

I remember graduating from Avonworth High School in Pittsburgh with such high hopes. But then about four years ago, I started asking myself questions like these: "What is missing in my life?" "Are the things I have experienced so far all there is to life?" "Is there anything in life that has a deeper meaning?"

I was overtaken by feelings of emptiness. At times I felt like I was living on an island all alone.

I began to reevaluate my life in an effort to understand and try to answer some of these questions. The more carefully I looked at things, the more I started to see the world changing around me.

I saw a society that was fueled by my generation—the baby boomer generation. Many of my contemporaries had achieved great material wealth, but we were losing our grip on more important things such as loving, caring, and kindness for one another.

As Michelle continued through her middle and high school years, I continued to see a big transformation and a decay of our educational systems. I felt we were losing our children. Like the baby boomers, it seemed that her generation was more focused on self than on the welfare of others. I was growing increasingly uncomfortable with a society that had great material wealth but was bankrupt when it came to caring for our young people or promoting people's spiritual growth.

After much soul searching, I realized that there were two major components missing from my life: my lack of giving to others and, most important, my connection with God. So in 1999 I began a journey to search and transform myself. But sadly, I continued to find myself just running in place and going back to status quo.

My real journey toward transformation began on April 20, 1999, the day of the Columbine shootings. I didn't realize at the time how much of an impact this day would have on my life, but now I can see that it did.

Like millions of people across America, I watched television that day with family and friends as the events unfolded at Columbine High School in Littleton, Colorado. As I stared in disbelief at the television as reporters detailed the horror and carnage of that event, I tried to imagine the pain and agony endured by residents of this suburban Colorado community.

We saw images of parents searching for their children and waiting and hoping that their loved ones were alive. Throughout the coming weeks we continued to watch and read media reports about this watershed event. Our hearts poured out to the families and victims of this incredible event as we watched funerals, wakes, and pain being delivered over the airways.

Out of all of this terror and tragedy came something that is still difficult for me to explain. The best way I can put it is to say that Columbine was like a divine calling that told me get up and do something constructive with my life. Columbine deepened my resolve to find some way to extend my reach to help others in need and establish a solid foundation of faith in my own life.

From that point on, my inner transformation began to have a greater sense of meaning and direction. I was fueled with a new energy to make a difference in our society. It was time for me to reach out and touch both youth and families.

Like most major changes in life, the road continued to be rocky at best. As I did more to help others, I really wasn't sure if I was making any difference. I continued to find myself on an emotional roller coaster ride. I felt defeated many times.

As far as faith, I wasn't seeing much change. I couldn't tell whether I was on the road to a gradual, ongoing progression or if my resolve had merely been something that hit me one moment but left me the next instant.

After two years of struggle, there was still something missing. I was looking for this somebody in my life to help me through my journey. Since working in our communities, I began to see many similarities to the Columbine incident. I saw young people showing lack of respect and care for each other. The Columbine tragedy was again something that continued to stay with me. However, I was feeling a compelling need to go behind the scenes and find a positive outcome to this tragedy so I could share it with others in our communities.

After hours of research, I found a Web site about one of the Columbine victims named Rachel Joy Scott. I spent hours reading about her in life and the deep devotion she had to help others through God. It was a moment in time that I finally found who I was looking for to help me through my journey. It was a person I knew in my heart who could really guide and help me to make a difference.

From there I took immediate action, and began reading *Rachel's Tears*, *Chain Reaction*, and a book about Rachel's journals. These incredible books changed my life forever. Here was a 17 year-old girl who was helping people in need, not wanting anything in return and trying to make this world just a better place.

Through her journals and amazing stories, it was like she was talking to me and providing me with a blueprint for success. Today I still keep these books with me as part of my daily life. You would think most people would just stop there, but I couldn't. I saw that Rachel's family was going across the country touching the lives of many people through the words of Rachel. It appeared to be a strong and powerful message that I needed to bring to our region. I knew at that time it was the connection I'd been looking for, a way to help others and to help us transform our community.

On September 30, 2001, some of us here in the Pittsburgh area hosted a community-wide event. Over 500 youth and adults came to St. Margaret Mary's Church in Moon Township to hear the story of Rachel's Challenge through the words of her older sister Dana.

She set the foundation by taking us back to April 20, 1999, [c]alling it ["]the worst day of my life." From there, she shared with us Rachel's words through her many journal entries and showed us how Rachel through her compassion was helping people at her school. She finished with an emotional mime routine based on the song "Watch the Lamb," similar to what she had done at Rachel's funeral, which we saw on CNN.

At the end of the program she received a standing ovation and we were so emotionally overwhelmed. Many in the audience were crying; they didn't want to leave.

During this event, Dana was awarded a proclamation from the [s]tate of Pennsylvania that declared the month of October as Random Acts of Kindness Month. We also produced a banner with a picture of Rachel Joy Scott that now hangs in government offices. We dedicated the entire program to Rachel Joy Scott and the other victims of Columbine and their families.

That event started us off with positive momentum as we visited five different school districts within the nearby Moon Area, Cornell Area, Montour Area, Ambridge Area, and Hopewell Area. In time, more than 5,000 students attended 10 different assemblies.

As she had before, Dana immediately connected with the students. Many of them cheered and clapped. It was amazing to see all the youth in the audience totally mesmerized by the videotape and each word Dana was saying about Rachel. You could have heard a pin drop in the auditoriums.

At each assembly the students gave her a standing ovation. After the program, many of the students came up to talk and they also shared their stories with Dana. Many of the students had read *Rachel's Tears* and *Chain Reaction*. Hearing Dana speak gave them a real connection to Rachel and her story.

My family and some of our friends had an opportunity to be with Dana and listen to many of the behind-the-scenes stories about how Rachel's passing was making an impact across the country for so many. It was amazing how one young person could have such a powerful impact on youth and adults.

It was that compelling week of emotion that brought me back to my faith in God.

After this week of events we received so many e-mails and letters about how these programs had started a "Chain Reaction" in our communities. Teachers and administrators were telling us how the climate in their schools was changing. They told us that they were witnessing Random Acts of Kindness being done throughout their schools between both youth and adults.

Other young people were turning toward God and beginning their faith journey. Many young people contacted us to perform volunteer service in our communities that extended our service offerings to more locations. But most of all, it brought youth together from various communities and school districts that started many positive friendships.

This was such an incredible feeling that we were able to touch so many lives in such a short period of time.

After that event I was such on an emotional high. However, several weeks later I was diagnosed with colon and rectal cancer. My journey through this illness has been an emotional roller coaster ride. However, because of my faith and this one incredible week, I am fighting this deadly disease and at peace with my life. I pray to God each and every day that Rachel Joy Scott, Dana Scott, and her family have come into my life to guide me toward my calling in life.

They have helped me move from success to significance toward Servant Leadership!

We continue to bring Rachel's messages back to our communities through her sister Dana. Dana has become one of our family and we are blessed that our lives have touched so many people.

It has been God's blessing that Rachel Joy's legacy continues to live through so many of us.

Now, I would like call out to both youth and adults across the world to make Rachel Joy Scott's legacy a part of their lives. I believe people who follow her example will be inspired by a young person whose example will encourage them to reach out and "Pay It Forward" through the grace of God.

Take a step and start a "Chain Reaction" in your own life and community, so that we can make this world a better place and promote continued acts of kindness toward each other.

(For more information about Don's work and ministry, please visit these Web sites: www.moonhelpline.com and www.careforyouth.org.)

Adults Caring for Kids

Like Don, many other adults have been inspired by Columbine and Rachel's story to reach out to youth in their own communities and schools.

Carrie L. Ostigaard, who is forty years old, is the women's ministries director at High Plains Christian Center in Strasburg, Colorado. Moved by the tragedy at Columbine, Carrie started simply by hosting a tea for the women in her church. The women who attended the event covered a wide age range: one was twelve years old, while others were in their seventies and eighties. But no matter how old they were, all were touched, and many decided to do something about it.

We asked Carrie to tell the story.

April 20th 1999, a day I will always remember. My husband Tim and I were watching television together that morning when our show was interrupted with a news story on Columbine. I sat there in terror and grief. We remained glued to the news programs for the rest of the day.

Tim and I have five children, and all but one were in school at the time. We looked at each other and asked, "How would we deal with this if it were one of our kids?"

Later, there were days when I would say to the Lord, "I know there is a reason for this tragedy, but how can good come out of something so terrible?"

I watched parts of Rachel's funeral on CNN. I can't explain what drew me to Rachel more than the other Columbine victims, but I believe it was because I sensed that we shared the same love for our Lord. Even more, I felt the Lord had a plan and He would use my family in this unfolding event.

I read everything on Columbine I could get my hands on. I read *Rachel's Tears* as soon as it came out. When I read Rachel's story, I was amazed at all the events that God set in motion and how He was turning it into a victory for Himself.

I never met Rachel, but I could tell she had a special place in the heart of Jesus. I wanted the relationship that she had. I had that relationship with the Lord when I was in my teens and I felt that I got too busy with life and ignored what Jesus really wanted for me. I was so into my own life that I would sometimes forget what a little reaching out to others can do for the kingdom of God.

I really believe that Rachel in her heavenly glory is dancing with Jesus and smiling at all that is happening in her family, school, and friends through her life and journals.

I told everyone I knew to read *Rachel's Tears*. One of the people I told was Lisa Johnson, a young single mom who attended Orchard Road Community Church. Dana Scott also attended Orchard Road and was a part of Lisa's small group.

As the women's ministry director at High Plains Christian Center, I organize our annual Ladies' Tea each spring. Soon, I decided that I would like Dana to speak at our next Ladies' Tea. Dana agreed to help us, [and] the event had the largest turnout we have ever seen.

A week after the tea, a Christian woman who knows some of the people on local school boards called me and asked if Dana would be willing to speak at some of the schools in our area. For me, this was a dream come true.

She called four school boards, and I talked to board members at a fifth school. Every school responded enthusiastically. Now, it looks like the doors are opening for Dana to speak at all five schools in our area! It is so awesome to me that something Tim and I had dreamed about for more than a year is coming to pass.

Working on this project, I have repeatedly seen that even though things might not always work out when and how we plan them, God sees the big picture. When He wants something to happen, He always makes things work out better than we could ever imagine and for His glory and the furtherance of his kingdom.

Tragedy can happen to any of us. It's what we do with tragedy that can change lives. Thank you, Dana and all the Scott family, for taking the legacy of your precious sister and daughter and using it to impact the world for Jesus!

Other Cities, Other Adults, Other Schools

I never know what's going to happen after I speak in a city, but thanks to a dedicated woman in Tracy, California, that city will always hold a special place in my heart. I was invited to speak there two times in one day. Mayor Dan Bilbrey, who was at both of those meetings, shared with me how Rachel had impacted his city.

It all started with a teacher named Linda Spaulding, who heard Rachel's challenge to start a chain reaction of kindness and compassion. Linda became consumed with a desire to change the city of Tracy by working with the elementary school children she taught. Because of her hard work, she was named her district's "character education coordinator." Here, in Linda's own words, is the story of what happened in Tracy.

Little did I know that my life would change because of a brief interview on the *Today Show*. It was Friday morning, April 20, 2001. I was getting ready for school, preparing for another day with my fourth graders at South/West Park School in Tracy, California.

I didn't realize that it was the 2-year anniversary of the Columbine tragedy until I turned on the TV. I was walking from my bathroom to my closet to pick out clothes, when I heard Ann Curry of the *Today Show* interviewing Darrell Scott, the father of one of the victims from Columbine.

Mr. Scott was talking about the new book he had written called *Chain Reaction*. It was based on his daughter's "Code of Ethics" that she had written a month before she was killed. What first captured my attention was the body language of the two people on the screen. The passion they displayed on the subject being discussed was so intense!

I was riveted to the screen as Mr. Scott began to quote from his daughter's writing: "I have this theory, that if one person can go out of their way to show compassion, then it will start a chain reaction of the same. People will never know how far a little kindness can go."

I grabbed a pencil and scribbled down the basic idea from the quote. I knew immediately that I was destined to do something with this. I felt a feeling within me that I could not explain as anything but a spiritual moment. I knew this was a catalyst for something important.

That morning in my first class a young girl, Allison, asked, "Mrs. Spaulding, did you know that this is the 2nd anniversary of the Columbine shooting?" I replied, "Yes, Allison, I do know that[;] in fact, let me tell you about one of the students who was killed that day." Now at this point I had not read the book Darrell Scott had written, and hardly knew anything about Rachel's life, but I launched out from the few words that had so powerfully motivated me earlier in the day.

As I talked about what I had heard and seen that morning on the *Today Show*, I found myself going over to the cupboard and getting several strips of colored construction paper. I cut the paper into one-inch strips while I continued to talk about Rachel's challenge to start a chain reaction.

"Here's what we're going to do," I said. "Every morning we'll take one of these strips of paper and we will write down something that someone has done for us that has made us feel good over the last 24 hours. It doesn't have to be big things[;] it can be little things like someone picking up something you dropped or someone saying something nice to you."

Little did I realize the enormous impact this small activity was going to have on the lives of so many people in our city! Something incredible began to happen! I began to hear them talk about their brothers and sister[s] saying "I love you." I began to hear them tell me that their mom[s] or dad[s] were helping them with different things. I began to get notes from moms and dads telling me that their kids were doing things at home they had never done before. I got notes saying that siblings were no longer fighting like they normally did.

We began to see a change on the school playground. We began to see them treat each other with more respect and kindness. There was an incredible change taking place, simply because they were focusing on the good things instead of the bad.

By the end of the year the news had gotten out concerning the transformation of the fourth graders. The chain reaction began to grow and find expression throughout the school district. I was asked to be the character education coordinator for our city at the end of the school year.

I began to take a copy of Rachel's essay and a lot of construction paper with me to every event. I spoke at staff meetings, service clubs, principals' meetings, educator training, and conflict management meetings. Everywhere

I spoke, Rachel's chain reaction was expanding. I soon became known as the "chain lady" among all the students. Soon there were chains everywhere, throughout the school district.

In April of 2002 we held our Second Annual Community Celebration of Character. Darrell Scott was our guest speaker. We hung chains around the room to let him know that we believe what Rachel said is true[:] "You never know how far a little kindness will go—you can start a chain reaction!"

Another teacher from Rockford, Michigan, tells of the project she launched after the Columbine killings rendered her and her seventh and eighth grade art students incapable of doing their normal work.

"They could not function," she writes. "None of us could." So the teacher and her coworker put the curriculum aside and tried to deal with the disaster creatively.

The students decided to assemble kits of the following: Seven one-yard pieces of embroidery thread would each stand for a specific value:

- Red: love
- Orange: faith
- Yellow: hope
- Green: growth
- Light blue: compassion
- Dark blue: trust
- Purple: courage

In addition, two beads—one gold and one silver—represented friends, old and new. A brass safety pin represented safety and a joining together. Everything was put together in a small, snack-size baggie along with a small piece of paper containing an explanation of the meanings of the various colors and materials as explained in Dag Hammarskjold's book *Markings*.

The kids went to work assembling the materials into kits, which they called "common threads." During the first three weeks of the project, they sold over 1,400 of them during their lunch hours at cost (50 cents each kit). The money was used to purchase more materials. Soon, word spread and kids from every social group were included. The materials the art students had assembled became a visible sign to others that meant "although we are different and unique, we still have certain values that we have in common that connect us."

Neighboring schools picked up on the idea, which was covered by the news media in the Grand Rapids area.

When superintendents from 20 surrounding school districts met to discuss strategies for the schools such as metal detectors, etc., our kids were asked to present their project.

Examples like this one and others I have heard demonstrate how Columbine was a powerful force in the lives of many. Perhaps we will never hear all the stories about the creative things people have done as a response.

Hope for Flawed, Fallen People

I have been a Christian for a long time. Over the years I have talked to many older believers who have experienced barren periods in their spiritual lives. A writer named Michael Yaconelli once described this predicament:

I want to introduce a new sociological category: failers. That is, people who fail on a regular basis. People like me.

I am a lay pastor of a small, not-growing church. I am not ordained. I am not seminary trained. I was asked to leave both Bible colleges I attended. I am divorced and remarried. On any given day I am capable of being a jerk with my wife and family. I am terminally insecure, which causes me to compensate with bouts of arrogance. At times people irritate me, and I hide from them. I am impulsive, which causes me to say things I shouldn't and make promises I cannot keep. I am inconsistent.

My walk with Christ is a stuttering, stumbling, bumbling attempt to follow Him. At times His presence is so real I can't stop the tears, and then, without warning, I can't find Him. Some days my faith is strong, impenetrable, immovable—and some days my faith is weak, pathetic, helpless, knocked about like a paper cup floating on the ocean in the middle of a hurricane.

I have been a Christian for 45 years. I am familiar with the vocabulary of faith, and I am often asked to give advice about matters of faith. But I am still a mess. I am light years away from being able to say with Paul, "Copy me." I am 56 years old and still struggling—a flawed, clumsy, unstable follower of Jesus. A bona fide failer.

That bothers a lot of people. Over the years they have expressed their displeasure with my failings. Some have abandoned me. Some have even written me out of the kingdom.

Not Jesus.

He refuses to give up on me. Sometimes, late at night, when I am just about to give in to sleep, I know I have heard Him weeping for me.

You see, Jesus has a fatal flaw: He can't stay away from failers. He is a friend of failers, a lover of failers. When everyone else has given up, He seeks them out—the woman who failed at five marriages; the blind man by the pool, who had failed to get his timing down for 38 years in a row; the woman with the blood disease, who failed at giving up; the disciple who failed at following; the fisherman who failed at fishing; the thief who failed at keeping the law; the adulterous woman who failed at moral purity; the doubting disciple who failed to believe.

Over the past three years, I have been surprised to hear from a number of confirmed "failers" who say Rachel's story has inspired spiritual renewal in their lives.

One twenty-nine-year-old woman from Shelbyville, Tennessee, said this:

Your story helped me to realize where I stand with God and it is nowhere close to where Rachel stood. I was raised in church my whole life and heard the gospel preached many times. I asked myself the question, Could I give my life for Christ? I sadly had to answer, "Maybe not." My heart ached so badly because I don't think I really could if it came down to it. I've been in and out of church so much and I'm only 29 and my life has not been close to making an impact on anyone's life. But if I could make an impact—even on one life— then my job here on earth and the trials I face would be so worth the fight.

A twenty-three-year-old man who works as a youth leader in his church in Maryland said Rachel's story helped him in other ways:

> Except for the Bible itself, no other book has ever impacted me the way *Rachel's Tears* did. Reading about your daughter's faith, the way she treated people, the way she acted—it really did help pull me out of a depression I was suffering last year. I didn't feel like I had a purpose here. It didn't seem like my life was going anywhere. I wasn't growing. *Rachel's Tears* was the kick I needed.

A forty-one-year-old father of three who lives on the East Coast heard a speech I had given after his wife purchased a taped copy of the talk. Here's what he said: "I have been walking away from God, or should I say, 'lukewarm.' I put in the tape and my daughter and I listened. I started crying. Your daughter's story broke my heart. She was a doer of the Word, not just a hearer and she strived to be unstained by the world. God was working on me before your talk, but hearing the tape hit me like a ton of bricks."

Having been a pastor myself, I know how tough it can be to live in a clergy family. That's why I was encouraged by this e-mail from Portland, New York: "I read *Rachel's Tears* from cover to cover in four hours. I am 40 years old, a pastor's wife, and she makes me feel so ashamed of my walk with the Lord. What wisdom and a relationship with Jesus she had."

And finally, a fifty-one-year-old man from the Rocky Mountain region where I live heard me on the radio: "I heard your message to teens on the Moody radio station tonight. My son was injured over the weekend and I've been in a low spot. You were a real encouragement to me. I have worked with teens in a church environment for 25 years. I know that teens at my church have been challenged by the stand that Rachel took, and adults, too."

God has a unique calling for each one of us, and it has been one of the joys of the past three years to hear from people how Rachel's example has encouraged them to find and follow their callings.

Examples like these show that Columbine and the spiritual revolution that came out of it is much more than kid stuff.

No matter how old you are or what kind of work and ministry you are involved in, God loves you and cares for you. If Rachel's story communicates that truth to you in a way that is meaningful and inspiring, I share your joy. And I'm sure she does, too.

Seven

Spiritual Light from a Dark Place

Some people believe that the killings at Columbine were so dark and evil that nothing good can ever come from them. Frankly, I can understand how they might think this.

But I have a different perspective, and it comes from hearing hundreds and hundreds of stories from people who say they have been touched and permanently transformed by the tragedy and its spiritual aftermath. If I wrote a book ten times longer than the one you hold in your hands, I couldn't even begin to share even a small percentage of the amazing stories people have told me.

There are stories about spiritual rebirth, like this one from a college student who was an atheist. Even though she didn't attend the event in her town where I spoke, she heard about it.

I want you to know that Rachel's story is changing the world we live in! I've been an atheist my whole life. I grew up around religious people and I made them miserable with my criticisms of a God who would create such a world as we live in. I was convinced that there was no such thing as a "personal relationship with God." I have never heard you speak, but you came to our campus recently and shared Rachel's story. Our college paper published the story and I read it a week after you were here. I was intrigued by what I was reading and I went to your Web site to find out more information.

I was completely shocked at the pictures Rachel drew and her writings. I could not get away from her story and I eventually bought a copy of *Rachel's Tears*, which totally blew me away! To make a long story short, I have now become a Christian, and I know what Rachel meant when she wrote about the "light that God had put in her." I believe with all my heart that her purpose on this earth was to live and die as a powerful testimony to people like me who may never come to know the powerful reality of Jesus Christ except through her story. Thank you so much for all you are doing to reach out to my generation through Rachel's life.

There are other stories from people who have been Christians for many years but experienced a spiritual renewal in the wake of Columbine. The following story from a pastor is one of those.

I am pastor of a Baptist church in north Alabama and will be preaching from Matthew 10:32-33 this Sunday morning. I would like to use the example of your daughter's stand for Christ as an illustration of what kind of commitment Jesus is calling for when He says for us to "confess Him before men." I am touched by this powerful testimony of Rachel, and am challenged to be stronger in my stand for Christ because of her.

I will never understand how God has used Rachel's story in so many powerful ways in the lives of so many people. It is one of the things I hope to understand better when I get to heaven myself.

In the meantime, I rejoice in the various ways God has shed spiritual light and truth from one of the darkest events of our time. I hope you can rejoice, too, as you read some of the following stories. And I pray that these stories will touch you and encourage you in your own spiritual walk.

A New Path in Life

For Kerry Koberg, the tragedy at Columbine helped inspire a spiritual rebirth that has set him on a new path in life. "God has planted a vision in my heart and soul to carry out and live a challenge from a girl I will never know in this life—Rachel Joy," he says. Here Kerry tells his own story:

In April of 1999 I was living in a tiny one-bedroom apartment in Cedar Rapids, Iowa[,] wondering what the true questions and answers of life were. It was near the end of my first year out of college. I found myself away from nearly everyone I knew and facing a lot of the questions 24 year-olds face. I had begun to grow dissatisfied with the road of life I seemed to find myself on. I found that even surrounded by "friends" in bars I would still experience complete and total emptiness on the inside. There was a hole inside me I couldn't fill.

Columbine wrecked me. I was devastated. I was captivated. Like everyone I had questions of how, why, and where were you, God?! I spent hours glued to Fox, CNN and the networks as they constantly aired coverage of Columbine. I watched the families, the friends, the classmates, the politicians, the rock stars, and the masses congregate on the hills, the churches, the parks, the malls, and the schools to hug, cry and share about Columbine. My heart was weeping more than it ever had. I had never experienced a loss like this. I didn't know the victims or the families of the victims, but it still hurt like nothing I can explain. Watching television, I would strum my guitar and cry out to God for answers. Something inside of me was dying and something inside of me was screaming to be heard.

Shortly after Columbine, shock rocker Marilyn Manson was coming to town for a concert. As you can imagine there was huge controversy surrounding this event due to the connection of his music to the killers. I didn't understand why, but I felt like I had to go to this show. My friends thought I was crazy and wouldn't go with me. So if I was going, I was on my own.

As I walked past a crowded street corner across from the event center I heard a voice call out to me asking if I wanted a piece of pizza. "No thanks," I said and kept walking. About four steps later a different voice called out, "Would you like a piece of pizza?" I froze. I stopped dead in my tracks and turned to look at two big brown eyes behind thick glasses staring intently and lovingly at me. She was part of a church group that was there praying for the kids and Marilyn and handing out free pizza and soda.

I immediately engaged her in conversation and we spent the rest of the night talking about Columbine, parents, and what causes kids to act out and search for meaning in ugliness and lies. She was in her early forties, a widow with three kids, and uncommonly on fire for God. She invited me to her church and over the next few weeks we had Bible studies and prayer together. I believe God used her and our time together to bridge the gap between my heart and my head.

Later that month I felt at peace as I awoke from a dream that told me to go to Columbine. I spent the rest of the month praying and putting the plan to action. My family and friends were a little worried about the sudden move, but I held firm to the vision and put my trust in God. On the first Sunday of June 1999 I packed my little Geo Prism full of stuff and set off on a journey to Denver, Colorado.

Once there I made my way to Clement Park next to Columbine High. I parked and strapped my guitar over my shoulder and walked to a picnic shelter where I sat and played the songs I knew and prayed to God. Then I walked up the hill where the 13 crosses had been erected. They were down now but I sat up there and looked down on Columbine High for the first time and in my own eyes saw this school that changed my heart and the hearts of millions.

My heart seemed to be growing as I stood there and prayed that God might use me, that He would forgive me for all the mistakes I'd made, and that He'd restore the life He'd given and use me for His glory. I was alone but I didn't feel alone. I had peace, I had JOY, and I had meaning.

Barely a year after Columbine, I was living in Denver and was invited by some new friends for an after-church feast of tostadas. As I was sitting on the floor with my plate resting on the coffee table, I looked through the glass and noticed the book *Rachel's Tears*. I grabbed the book and flipped through its pages. I asked who owned the book, and they said, "It's our roommate Dana's." "Who's Dana?" I asked. "Dana is Rachel's sister," they said. It was like someone punched me in the stomach as I searched for the air to breathe. Even in my humanity and screw-ups throughout the past year God had brought me to where I needed to be.

I always knew Columbine was more than a tragedy. I don't know why this event and this little girl touch me so deep[ly], but the more I learn about Rachel Joy Scott through her family and friends confirms to me that in some unexplainable way she has given me life through her death. That is why I am so determined to make sure the principles she stood for carry on in her memory. Rachel and I have a lot in common—from our personalities to our longing for a deep, honest spiritual walk. We both have a desire and a willingness to connect with people in odd and unconventional ways. There is also a passion for people and a recognition of how the little things of life truly make all the difference. Simple things, like giving a stranger a smile, helping a friend in need, loving on people, and definitely not taking ourselves too seriously.

I am inspired by the life of Rachel Joy and believe that I have my very own angel encouraging me every step of the way. Her struggles, her moments of glory, her wisdom, her love, and her seeking of the true God push me on in my own walk. Rachel Joy Scott showed me a life where faith and honesty and love are all possible. She spoke of starting a "chain reaction" of kindness and of loving one another unconditionally and seeing what a better place this world could be if we could do these little things. Rachel's Challenge is so simple, yet so profound.

Today, as I sit at Rachel's grave and look at the crosses of each of the 13 lives that were taken, I am at peace that these lives were not lost in vain.

"I won't be labeled as average!" That was Rachel's cry and it is the cry of her generation. It is my cry as well. In reflection on the past couple years of my life, I am humbled at the things God has allowed me to see and do. God has been faithful in providing the gifts and talents to live an amazing life. I have a daily opportunity to continue living out the creed Rachel Joy stood for. It is something I cherish. With opportunities through music to reach young people and encourage them to hope, to dream, to love, to be different, and to put their faith in God, I am able to continue carrying the torch Rachel lit three years ago. I hope someday to meet her in heaven and hang out with her for a while. That will be so cool! As she would affectionately sign off in her journals and letters, ♥ Always, Rachel Joy. So true. Love Always. Love Always.

The Joys of Temptation

It's not easy being a Christian young person today. Temptations seem to lurk from nearly every corner. Sexual temptations have always been a struggle for Christians, but in our own day, movies, TV commercials, and Internet sites are overflowing with sexual images that would have shocked earlier generations of believers. Drugs and alcohol have also been perennial temptations, but it seems that these temptations are more readily available in schools than they were when I was student.

Rachel faced the typical challenges and temptations of every teenager. She felt the same peer pressures that all of us have struggled with during our middle and high school years. She experienced ups and downs and also had her share of both victories and failures.

In her journals, Rachel confessed her struggles and temptations about sex and alcohol with amazing openness and transparency. She recorded one of her bouts with temptation in her diary on April 15, 1998. This was one year and five days before her death. Here's what she wrote:

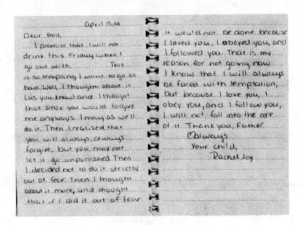

I have been deeply moved by her total honesty with herself and with God every time I read this portion of her diary. You can see her walking through the process of temptation in her mind and watch her come to certain conclusions that ultimately led her to make the right choice.

If you look carefully at what Rachel wrote, you can see that there is a process to how she dealt with temptation that can help all of us when we are tempted.

First, she was honest about the things she confronted. Rachel was truthful in saying, "This is so tempting. I want to go so bad." There are many times when most of us aren't this honest with God and ourselves about wrong desires.

Second, she had no doubt that God loved her and would forgive her no matter how many times she failed. Many of us don't really have that kind of security and faith in God's grace.

Third, she admitted that she was tempted to take advantage of God's grace and His promise to forgive our faults and failures. In a sense, this was her second temptation. The first was to go out and drink. The second was to take advantage of God's grace.

Fourth, she addressed the issue of fear of punishment. "I realized that you will always, always forgive, but you may not let it go unpunished." She understood that even though God is faithful to forgive, she could still reap consequences from her wrong choices.

Finally, she examined her own motive for obedience. Is it from fear or from love? "If I did it out of fear it would not be done because I loved you, I obeyed you, and I followed you."

In the end, Rachel made the right decision for the right reason, "because I love you, I obey you, and I follow you." She closed her journal entry with thanksgiving to God for helping her do the right thing.

Even though this episode takes up only a few pages of *Rachel's Tears*, we have many e-mails and comments from young people about this passage in her diary. The following e-mail from a high school girl was sent in October of 2000. I'm sure it would have brought a smile to Rachel's face:

I would like for you to know I was on a bus full of softball athletes (including myself) the other day and half of them are not Christians (true) yet they believe in the existence of God but they are not devoted and are very lost in that area. Though they are my friends.

They took the book (*Rachel's Tears*) from me and started reading all the things Rachel wrote in her diary. The one that hit them the most was the one about her temptation to drink. She said even though she wanted to go, even though God would forgive her afterwards, she loved Him and wasn't going to go. One girl said, "Hey, I wish I had an attitude like that!" Another told me, "I want to go with you to church Sunday." I just wanted to let you know how much one little entry changed their way of thinking. They kept reading and reading and a lot of them started realizing that she loved God so much and just everything. I wanted to tell you this and thank you and your family for writing that book. If only we can learn more from Rachel and your family. They have a waiting list of who gets the book after I read it.

It may seem strange that people are reading and reacting to things written in Rachel's private journal. On the other hand, Rachel wanted God to use her and wrote that often in her diaries. She once wrote, "I want them to see the light you have put in me." Sometimes that light shone in ways she never suspected. Sometimes it isn't our strengths that help others; it is our weaknesses. God's grace is made perfect through our weakness.

The same day we received the e-mail above, a young man e-mailed us about the impact Rachel had on his life. He had been amazed that she was willing to confide that she had given in to the temptation to try smoking.

I am reading *Rachel's Tears* and I attended a "Call to All" rally where your daughter Dana talked. I am very sorry about Rachel, but I wanted you to know, though you probably get this all the time, that she was an amazing inspiration to me. I was sinning against my parents for a while and I talked to them about it the other day, thinking of when Rachel told you about smoking and the speeding ticket. I just wanted to thank you and Mrs. Nimmo for writing that book. I am praying for you and your family.

Being Thankful for Temptation?

All of us experience temptation in our lives. But surprisingly, James, the half brother of Jesus, wrote in James 1:2 that we should "consider it pure joy" when we fall into different temptations.

How can he say such a thing? It seems strange to rejoice when we are tempted. The natural reaction is to hide the fact that we are tempted by pretending that the temptation doesn't exist or to go to the other extreme and secretly indulge our passions and desires.

But celebrate with joy? Hardly! And yet, that is exactly the formula for success in the midst of temptation. Most of us don't obey James' command to rejoice when we are tempted because that doesn't make sense to us. I think part of what James is trying to tell us is that temptation is a necessary part of our spiritual growth. It is the only way we will ever become spiritually mature and partake fully of God's divine nature through His "very great and precious promises" (2 Peter 1:4).

But promises aren't enough by themselves! They must go through a process to be converted into provisions in our life, and part of the process includes temptation.

This spiritual principle can be explained through the use of four important words:

- Promises
- Principle
- Problem
- Provision

God gave Israel wonderful *promises* in the Old Testament. He promised them a land flowing with milk and honey (abundance). He promised them wells they didn't dig, vineyards they didn't plant, and houses they didn't build! He then gave them the key, the *principle* that would convert those promises into *provisions*. He said, "If you are willing and obedient, you will eat the good of the land."

Next came the *problem*: a wilderness that lay between them and the *promised* land. All they had to do was apply the *principle* (willingness and obedience) in the midst of the *problem* (wilderness) to inherit the *provision* (Canaan!). But they refused and rebelled and murmured and complained for forty years, and although they were God's people, many of them perished in the wilderness simply because they refused to be thankful in the middle of the testing!

It only took Jesus forty days to go through His wilderness experience. It took Israel forty years! Our extended stay in the wilderness depends on our ability to apply the *principle* in the midst of the *problem* to convert the *promise* into a *provision*!

When Jesus was tempted He didn't murmur or complain. He showed an "attitude of gratitude in the restriction of affliction" and simply stood in faith on the promises of God. Forty days later He emerged out of that wilderness experience in the "power of the Spirit" (Mark 4:14). He entered into the *provision* of all that the Father had given Him.

The real purpose of temptation is to reveal what was already in our heart. Many times we don't know things are there until God's special "ways and means" committee designs problems especially suited to our individual character development! We can "consider it all joy, my brethren, when you encounter various trials" (James 1:2 NASB) if we understand that trials are simply an opportunity to grow through right choices. We can give thanks for the temptation when we realize that a sovereign God has allowed us into a situation that exposes something in us that needs to be dealt with.

The next time you are tempted with lust or something else, simply begin to thank God for the fact that what was really in your heart has been exposed, and watch the lust disintegrate! Rachel understood these things and was able to communicate them in such a way that they would impact other young people, even after her death. Rachel had learned this principle from a book written by Bob Mumford, called *The Purpose of Temptation*. Bob wrote the foreword to the book you're now reading. He has been a true inspiration to our family for many years.

Other Struggles and Trials

Temptation is only one of the struggles we face in our spiritual lives. For some people, one of the biggest battles they encounter is the decision about whether or not to give their lives to God.

We regularly receive testimonies from people who say Rachel helped them decide to follow Christ. One of these came from a fifteen-year-old high school student who shared the following story:

> On April 20, 1999, I was sitting in my sixth period class. I was listening to a CD I had recently purchased: Marilyn Manson's *AntiChrist Superstar*.
>
> Over the blaring of the CD, I heard a gasp go through our classroom as the students in my class saw a news report about the Columbine massacre on TV.
>
> That weekend, I was scheduled to go on a youth retreat for my school (my parents forced me to go). When I arrived at the conference center, I had only one thought on my mind: "Get me out of here, I'm bored."
>
> The theme of the conference was an anti-hate message. Throughout the three days of the conference, Columbine was the main topic of discussion. I was still hating being there. On the third day though, I learned of two victims: Cassie Bernall and Rachel Joy Scott. In Rachel's smile, I saw what I had always been before something happened that killed everything good inside of me. In Cassie's, I saw my Christian faith that was lost long ago.
>
> On the third night, right before we left, I went to the Chapel. I was carrying three things. Two pictures: one of Rachel, one of Cassie, and the Marilyn Manson CD I had purchased just a week earlier. I fell to my knees before the cross with the pictures in my hand, and broke the CD into as many pieces as it would break into. I prayed that the world would learn to love instead of hate, to advance life instead of kill, and I prayed to feel God's love again in my life.
>
> In a way, Columbine SAVED a life—mine. The only reason I am sitting here today was that your daughter's faith proved to me that there IS a God and that it is possible to live after tragedy.
>
> In my school, I am in a "group" similar to Columbine's "trenchcoat mafia" that included Eric Harris and Dyan Klebold. But there is a major difference— we DON'T kill people. We are simply banded together to help each other since

everyone else shuns us. We are not angry, or lonely, or sad. We just express ourselves. Don't judge everyone you see who is wearing all black clothing. They need to be loved too. Your daughter's faith and ability to stand saved my life.

Another testimony came from a mother who lives on the West Coast: "One of the girls in my daughter's youth group who had been considering trusting Christ for her salvation and life for quite some time but [was] unable to commit, gave her heart to Him after your presentation. My own daughter came back with your talk being the foremost thing in her memory. Her own faith was boosted by Rachel's faithfulness to her Lord."

Another e-mail came to us from a student in Nova Scotia:

The main reason I want to write is to describe the impact Rachel's story had on me, and how it changed my life completely. For nine years, I wandered. For nine years, I was lost, I was miserable. There was so much about me that I just didn't like, and didn't know how to change it. As a result, I became one of the most hateful people you would ever have the misfortune to meet.

Rachel's story was a life-changing experience. God used Rachel to guide me home to Him. I am eternally grateful for that, and I have never been happier.

Stories of Renewal

I'm thankful that Rachel's story has helped so many people experience a life-changing relationship with Christ. For others, Rachel's example has resulted in a stronger and more active faith.

Here's what one high school student had to say:

I had been going to a youth group for a year and a half and about there things started going bad for me. I got mad at God for the horrible things that were taking place in my life and I just gave up on Christianity and even burned my Bible. My youth pastor's message was about "Walking Your Talk" and Rachel Scott your daughter. At first I was like, "Whatever[;] another wasted night."

I sat there and listened to the fateful story about your amazing daughter. Thanks to your daughter's story I am back on my pursuit to live up to Rachel's standards.

A fifteen-year-old student from Dade City, Florida, had this to say:

After hearing Darrell's message, I was so touched that day. It has totally changed my life and my relationship with God SO much. I never really witnessed as often as I should have at school or otherwise and, at the time, my life was starting to get twisted around. I realized that I wasn't living for Him as much as I should.

On April 20, 2000, I was given several opportunities to witness to friends of mine who had asked me the day before if I was going to go to school the next day or not. I proudly said, "Yes" and told them, "What is meant to be will be, and if I'm meant to die for Christ, it's worth it and God will give me the courage to get through it."

After that they would ask me why [it] would be worth it, which opened the door for even more opportunities to share God.

A mother from Georgia reported on Rachel's similar impact on her daughter's life:

When you asked the young people to gather around the crosses, my daughter nearly knocked me down getting out of the aisle. Three years ago, she had decided that life was not worth living, and attempted to take her own life. We got into therapy, but nothing really seemed to help. She was overweight, didn't have a lot of friends, and had no self-esteem. For the last year, my daughter has been having doubts about her faith, what she believes, if she believes anything. She has attended church all her life. When you talked about starting a chain reaction in your school, her heart was touched. She told me that she wanted to be like Rachel. She wanted to start a chain reaction, she wanted people to look at her and ask what it was that made her different. She began witnessing to her friends and coworkers.

She later told me that she had heard "preaching" all her life, but, actually, finally "heard" when you spoke.

Three other testimonies describe how young people were inspired to take a stronger stand for their faith after Columbine:

I have been inspired by your daughter to take a stand for Christ. I have always been a Christian, but I also wanted to keep God in a box, so to speak[,] and only take him out on Sundays.

After realizing that many children, including your daughter, have taken a stand for Jesus, I, too, have decided to take a stand.

Out of all the people who died, it seemed that Rachel stood out the most for me. I didn't know then, but I do know now why. Through her, God was sending me a message. I am Catholic and went to Catholic school for 12 years. We had to go to church every day, so by the time I got to college I was burned out. Plus, I didn't believe a lot of what the Catholic church was teaching. I was torn. I still believed in God, but I didn't know how to express myself to him. That's where Rachel comes into play in my life. After reading *Rachel's Tears*, I called a Christian church in St. Louis where I plan on going.

I also plan on keeping a journal like Rachel. She has helped me to realize that it's what is inside the person that counts and not what's on the outside. Just today as I was walking to school, I saw a homeless person and not only did I give him $5.00, but I talked to him for 10 minutes. I would never have done that if I didn't read Rachel's book. After I read the book, I bought 5 more copies to give my friends.

I spent all my days in Barnes and Noble or Borders reading books about Columbine. One of the books I bought I already finished reading was *Rachel's Tears*. It was the most moving book I have ever read and it brought me to tears more than once. I wish I could express to you how much that book has changed my life. Before reading this book I was questioning my faith. I was raised in a very religious family but I was still questioning the existence of God as Rachel did a few times. After reading the book I feel so much better than before. I want to become a better Christian. Rachel is the best role model that I have ever had. I have started to treat ALL people with kindness. I want to start a chain reaction just like Rachel did.

What Will You do?

Columbine has impacted so many people in so many different ways. A woman named Lisa Johnson wrote the following story, which challenges all of us to respond to the challenge Rachel has given us.

April 20th, 1999 will be etched in my memory forever. I was at work in Englewood, Colorado, and I remember hearing about what was going on at Columbine High School over the radio.

I sat there in shock, while we watched the events unfold, again, and again on TV. I remember thinking, how would I feel if this was my son? My relief for the time came from the fact that my son goes to school up in Wyoming. I called that day, as soon as his school was out[,] just to hear his voice.

As the events unfolded, and the names started to emerge of kids that were confirmed dead, and kids that were injured, the sense of compassion [and] empathy that I felt was almost suffocating. I felt undeserving that at the touch of a keypad, I could talk to my son immediately and hear his voice.

In September 1999, I was in a very serious horse riding accident, and was taken via Flight-for-Life to a head-trauma unit in a hospital in Denver. I remember reading in my journal afterwards entries made a couple of days before my accident. I was really examining my life due to the events at Columbine, and if I was to die today, would I be OK with that? Did I know for sure that I'd go to heaven? What would I do differently if I knew I was going to die? What would I be doing right now? If I knew, how would that change my life? However, I was OK with dying, and I knew beyond a shadow of a doubt I would go to heaven.

Through the many things that have happened since Columbine, God has been challenging us to move the focus off of ourselves, and broaden our view. Holding the door for a pregnant lady who had her arms full[;] smiling at the person you passed on the street[;] throwing away someone else's trash that was left at the restaurant [where] you had just eaten[;] answering the store clerk who says "Hi, how are you?"[;] saying "Hi" everyday to the quiet person at the office. These things cost so very little! Some go unnoticed, some do not. You never know what kind of impact the little things have or what kind of door of opportunity it could open up.

Rachel's impact is something I will be changed by for the rest of my life. It wasn't just a one-time event. Her challenges from God, and insights into what God had for her and the rest of us, are things I have grafted into my everyday life. God sent His only son to die on a cross for us, as a free gift, to erase all the junk/sins we've gotten into. I feel like sometimes God is stopping to ask us, what have you done with the gift I sent you? Though Rachel's life was taken in the midst of an evil event, God has turned it around and used it for His ultimate recognition/glory.

I feel like God has given the world a gift through the published insights and writings from Rachel's journals (parents and family as well) in her relationship with God. What have I done with that gift?

I like the question Lisa asks. What have you done with all the things God has given you? How will you respond to His love and mercy?

For whatever reason, God in His wisdom has chosen to use Rachel to challenge many people with such questions. How will you respond to the challenge that has been offered?

Eight

The Son of Sam
and the Son of God

O ver the past three years, we have received thousands and thousands of letters and e-mails from people who write to tell us about the impact Rachel has had on their lives. In addition, many people have posted their thoughts on hundreds of Web sites. Some of these Web sites are dedicated to Rachel or Columbine, while others are people's home pages with sections devoted to Rachel.

It is always fascinating to read these letters and postings. I am continually amazed and pleased at the many ways Rachel's message has gone out and been received by people from all parts of the world and all walks of life.

But I have to admit that some of the most unusual communication we have had has been with a man named David Berkowitz. As you will see, this exchange, which has continued for the past year and a half, has been a unique testimony not only to Rachel's work but also to the power of Jesus to heal and forgive even the most desperate of sinners.

A Posting from David

Someone had told me that David had written some comments about the impact Rachel's message had on his life. Here's what that one posting, dated February 28, 2001, said:

> I want to briefly talk about a special book which has touched my heart and has given me a great deal of inspiration. I have read it through two times, and I occasionally open it up at random to read several pages.
>
> The name of the book is *Rachel's Tears: The Spiritual Journey of Columbine Martyr Rachel Scott* (Thomas Nelson Publishers, Nashville, Tennessee, ©2000). This book was written by Rachel's parents, Beth Nimmo and Darrell Scott.
>
> And as most people probably know, Rachel was a young woman who was one of thirteen people who lost their lives when two other students entered the Columbine High School in Littleton, Colorado, and opened fire on their classmates. Both of the gunmen also died.
>
> This happened on April 20, 1999. Almost everyone knows the facts. I don't think anyone knows all the reasons. It was a tragedy.
>
> But once again, God's hands of love have moved in this situation, and He has already brought many good things out of this sad event.
>
> Rachel's parents have, with God's gentle guidance, turned their grief into positive channels. It was also so obvious to me that Rachel's writings are anointed by the Holy Spirit.

From the outset of this tragedy many other students at Columbine plus people all over the world have come to Christ for salvation as a result of all the sermons that have been preached. This book, in my opinion, is one of the most important books to be published. I would encourage others to read it.

D.B.

Good News from an Unusual Source

I read the letter with unusual interest because I knew who David Berkowitz is. Maybe you have never heard of him, but he is well-known around the world by his nickname: "The Son of Sam."

Perhaps that name rings a bell in your memory. If not, I'll tell you who David is. He is one of the best-known serial murderers of the twentieth century. For more than a year he went on a bloody killing spree that held the entire city of New York in a state of fear. His story has been told in books, a movie, and hundreds of articles.

I don't want to glorify his criminal career, but I do want to briefly recap some of what he did and why he became so feared and infamous. By understanding where this man came from, we can come to a deeper understanding of the infinite love and mercy of our God.

Memoir of a Murderer

David Falco was born June 1, 1953, but was soon given up for adoption and was subsequently adopted by Nathan and Pearl Berkowitz, a Jewish couple from New York.

He graduated from Christopher Columbus High School in the Bronx and attended Bronx Community College for one year before joining the army in 1971. He flunked his first rifle-shooting test, but worked on improving his marksmanship, eventually becoming an infantry sharp-shooter with the M-16 rifle. While in the army he also turned his back on the Jewish upbringing he had received from his adoptive parents.

Not much was heard from Berkowitz over the next few years. He worked as a mail sorter in a New York post office and apparently lived a quiet and solitary life that drew little attention or respect.

Then, on July 29, 1976, Berkowitz began the killing spree that would make "Son of Sam" a feared and despised household name. He fired into a car in which two young women were sitting. The shots killed Jody Valent and seriously injured her friend.

Next, Berkowitz followed this by shooting Carl Denaro while the man was sitting in a parked car with his girlfriend. Miraculously, Denaro was not killed even though he sustained gunshot wounds to the head. His girlfriend was not injured.

In November 1976, Berkowitz opened fire on two young women at nearly point-blank range. Both managed to survive, though one was paralyzed.

For more than a month, Berkowitz was quiet. Then in early 1977, he continued his murderous rampage. In January he killed Christine Freund while she sat in a car in Queens with her boyfriend, who survived. On March 8, he shot and killed Virginia Voskerichian, and on April 17 he murdered a couple parked in their car in a secluded lover's lane.

In this case, Berkowitz left a letter at the scene of the crime. In the letter, he taunted the police and promised to strike again. The letter was signed "Son of Sam." This was the first time people had a nickname to attach to the murderer in their midst.

By this time, the entire city of New York was on edge. People knew a murderer was at large in their city, and they were screaming for an arrest to be made. The police made a desperate effort to find the Son of Sam, eventually assigning 75 detectives and 225 uniformed cops to work full-time on the case. Another 700 of New York's finest volunteered to work on the case during their off-duty hours. In all, these law enforcement personnel sought information on leads concerning 1,500 different potential suspects.

But Son of Sam eluded the police dragnet for another four months of killing and psychological terror.

On June 26, 1977 he opened fire with his 44-caliber gun outside of a Queens nightclub, injuring a couple while they sat in their car. A short time after, he shot at another couple kissing in a car. Stacy Moskowitz later died from a head wound, but her boyfriend surprisingly survived.

At the time, New York City was suffering through a record-breaking heat wave with temperatures that rose above 100 degrees. People were suffocating in the humid summer heat, but many were afraid to leave their houses at night or even open windows and doors, for fear that they would become the Son of Sam's next victim.

But Berkowitz had made a silly mistake that would lead to his arrest. He typically drove his own 1970 Ford Galaxy sedan to the areas where he planned his murders and used the car for his getaways. But at the site of the Moskowitz attack he got a parking ticket. This gave the police the crucial piece of information they needed, linking Berkowitz to the killings. They arrested the killer outside his Yonkers apartment on August 10, 1977.

"Inspector, you finally got me," he said as he was handcuffed and placed in a police cruiser. "I guess this is the end of the trail."

Before his surprising capture, Berkowitz had shot thirteen different people in eight separate nighttime attacks. Six of these victims died. The other seven survived, though one was blinded and one was paralyzed for life.

With Berkowitz's arrest, the Son of Sam's crime spree had ended. But this was just the beginning of a more bizarre part of the story. Over the next few months, Berkowitz divulged the details of his crimes. Soon, people all over New York and throughout the world would have an unprecedented glimpse into the troubled mind and twisted soul of a serial killer who had wreaked so much havoc and spilled so much innocent human blood.

And as we will see, it is this troubled mind and twisted soul that have now been healed and cleansed by the blood of Jesus.

A Glimpse into One Man's Sick Soul

A flood of newspaper and magazine articles covered the arrest and the details that emerged from days of interrogation. *Time* magazine devoted significant portions of its August 15 and August 22, 1977, issues to the story.

"He talked readily about his crimes," said one *Time* article, "showing amazing recall of each attack, correcting police on details that only he could know, never refusing to answer their impatient questions."

When asked why he had murdered, Berkowitz gave a confusing and convoluted explanation. "It was a command," he said. "I had a sign and I followed it. Sam told me what to do and I did it. He told me to kill. Sam is the Devil."

Berkowitz's Sam was either a next-door neighbor or a "man who lived

6,000 years ago." And Sam communicated his orders to Berkowitz through a black Labrador retriever named Harvey.

Berkowitz was found guilty or multiple murders and sentenced to 364 years in prison. Today he is prisoner number 78-A-1976 at the Sullivan Correctional Facility in Fallsburg, New York. He will most likely die in prison, as he is serving out his sentence.

And it's a good thing police caught the killer, because he was growing tired of merely murdering one or two people at a time. At the time of his arrest he was planning a more daring and dastardly attack. He had purchased a semiautomatic rifle and said he planned to drive out to the fashionable Hampton resort communities on Long Island and blast away at a crowd in a discotheque or nightclub. He was ready, he said with a smile, "to go down in a blaze of glory."

Thankfully, things didn't turned out as Berkowitz planned. He did experience glory, but not in the sense he had planned. Instead, God's glory came to him in his prison cell.

A Relationship Begins

Over the years I had heard that David Berkowitz, the Son of Sam, had become a Christian while serving his six consecutive life sentences behind bars.

Like most people, I was somewhat skeptical, knowing that sometimes prisoners will fake their conversions to a religion just to try and lighten their sentences, or to get out of prison sooner. However, in David's case, that really wouldn't apply, because there is no way he will ever be released from his imprisonment.

I had also heard that he had read and was impacted by *Rachel's Tears*.

Shortly after hearing that he had read the book, I wrote a letter to David. He responded immediately with a posting on his Web site, dated April 16, 2001:

The mail is usually passed out by the cell block guard at about 4:15 every afternoon, Monday thru Friday. In here a corrections officer would go from cell to cell handing each inmate his mail.

But as I thumbed through the six or so letters I got today, as soon as I saw one particular return address, I froze. I was completely stunned. I even started talking to myself out loud, asking why someone like this person would write me. I'm serious!

This person was Darrell Scott, the father of Columbine High School martyr, Rachel Joy Scott. I never wrote to him before, and I had no idea this man even knew that I existed. Plus, it is so ironic because just a few months earlier I had written in my journal for February 28th how very blessed I was by the book both Darrell Scott and his former wife, Beth Nimmo[,] had written together about their daughter.

Apparently someone told Mr. Scott that I was encouraged by Rachel's story. He said that he had heard about my coming to Christ "some time ago" and that he was "thankful" for what God has done in my heart.

Only the Lord Jesus could grant all this mercy to me that I would find favor with someone like Darrell Scott.

Furthermore, in his short letter he asked me if I had been forgiven by any of my victims' families. He also asked if I had developed any relationships with some of them.

I found it amazing that he would ask this when it has been one of the biggest cries of my heart that the forgiveness he is talking about would one day become a reality. So many of my brethren have been praying for these very same things: healing, salvation, forgiveness.

D.B.

Berkowitz responded by writing me a letter, which I received a few days later. The return address on the envelope I was holding read, "Sullivan Correctional Facility." I immediately knew who had written it.

It came from the man who had terrorized New York City more than anything or anyone ever had until September 11, 2001, the man who had given himself over to demonic influences and will forever be remembered alongside the names of Ted Bundy and Jeffrey Dahmer.

It was with some apprehension that I opened David's letter and began to read. The first thing I was struck by was what seemed to be genuine humility. David expressed his concern for how I might receive a letter from him and then shared about how Rachel's story had deeply touched his heart.

He extended an invitation to meet with him should I ever speak in the area near the prison. He then exposed his heart and his regret for his own deeds of twenty-four years earlier, when he had been the source of pain to parents like myself.

Here is the text of his letter:

David Berkowitz #78-A-1976
Sullivan Correctional Facility
P.O. Box 116
Fallsburg, NY 12733-0116

Dear Mr. Scott,

When I was handed your letter during the 4:15 mail call, I was totally stunned when I saw your name and address. I was simply amazed that you would write to someone in my situation. I felt unworthy to even read your letter, and I feel so unworthy answering it.

My heart goes out to you at your loss.

Your daughter's life and testimony has been such a great encouragement to me. I have read *Rachel's Tears* several times. Her life and even her death have been used by the Lord to bring many thousands into the everlasting kingdom.

Even now the Lord has been giving Rachel the desires of her heart to be a full time missionary and soul winner in many "unconventional" ways.

Being that tomorrow happens to be the anniversary of the Columbine tragedy, I plan to set aside the day in prayer and fasting, praying for the youth of our nation.

Mr. Scott, to answer your questions, it is somewhat ironic that you would ask me about being forgiven by the victims' families, or if I have developed any relationships with them. For unknown to you, this is one of the biggest desires on my heart.

In fact only a short time ago I sent to a pastor two letters for two different families in the New York City area. He has been praying on what to do next and how to approach these parties. [The Pastor] has been waiting on the Lord to direct him. Do you have any suggestions?

Furthermore, a couple in Georgia who are dear Christian friends of mine have been in touch with [one of the victim's mothers]. They have become close friends to her.

I cannot imagine how much pain, anger and bitterness the families have towards me. They have every right to feel these things. I am so sorry for what happened [nearly] 25 years ago. I pray in Jesus' name that they will all be able to heal from this tragedy and get on with their lives as best as possible.

D.B.

The Struggle to Forgive

After reading his letter, I made some phone calls to a number of people who had met with Berkowitz throughout the years. Every single one of them encouraged me to meet with him and confirmed that his encounter with God was a genuine thing. I made a mental note to keep an open mind about a possible meeting with him.

As a Christian, I knew that God's forgiveness was real. I had experienced that forgiveness in my own life many times and had learned the value in forgiving others. But forgive someone who had murdered six people! Could God really change a heart that far gone?

It's so easy to theorize and contemplate abstract truths such as love, compassion, forgiveness, and grace. It's a totally different thing to be confronted by one of these abstracts that has become powerful reality and to then know how to respond!

In Rachel's "Code of Ethics" she had challenged her readers to start a chain reaction through compassion. She listed five ingredients that, to her, defined compassion. The first of those five ingredients was forgiveness.

Our family was confronted with this issue shortly after her death. We could choose to be angry, bitter, and unforgiving, or we could turn to God's grace for the strength to forgive and refuse to be victimized twice over. It is a natural reaction to harbor anger and unforgivingness toward those who have harmed or destroyed the ones we love. It requires turning to a greater source than ourselves to truly forgive.

Individually and separately each one of us in Rachel's family chose forgiveness. We all understood that the alternative choice would only lead to bitterness, anger, rage, and possibly extended violence.

Pardon Versus Forgiveness

We also understood that forgiveness is not the same as pardon.

In the book *Chain Reaction*, I addressed the difference between pardon and forgiveness. Pardon and sentencing have to do with actions. Eric Harris and Dylan Klebold were responsible for their horrible actions and, had they lived, should have suffered the consequences of those actions. We would have seen to it that they were prosecuted and not set free to continue inflicting pain and suffering on others. But at the same time, we could not allow ourselves to harbor hatred and unforgivingness toward them.

Forgiveness is not a natural or human trait. It is a divine gift that is needed more by the one offended than by the offender. It is an issue of the heart. All of us have been on both ends of this issue. We have all needed forgiveness and we have all needed to forgive. Jesus understood this, and in the Lord's Prayer, He instructed us to pray, "Father ... forgive us our debts as we also have forgiven our debtors" (Matt. 6:9,12).

And now I was reading a letter from a man who had committed atrocities on the same level that Eric and Dylan had. Forgiveness where Eric and Dylan were concerned was an issue I didn't have to continue struggling with, because they died the same day as Rachel.

Once God's grace enabled me to forgive, it was not an ongoing struggle with people who were still alive, but now I was confronted with a different issue. I was in communication with a man who had killed others and who was still around. I wondered how I would react to David Berkowitz if I ever actually met him. It wouldn't take long for me to find out.

A Meeting in the Cell Block

In March of 2002 I was asked to speak at Cornell University and Ithaca College, both located in Ithaca, New York. I also received an invitation from people who work with prison ministries to join them in a meeting with David Berkowitz.

Early one morning we got in our car and set out for the Sullivan Correctional Facilities. As we drove up before the cold, harsh walls topped by razor-sharp loops of barbed wire, with armed guards posted at high points around the prison, my heart was pounding. Were we going to meet with a slick con-man who was pretending to be a Christian for his own self-interests, or were we going to meet a truly changed man who had experienced the divine forgiveness of God's grace? Cunning con or true Christian?—that was the question in my mind.

After being searched and passing through metal detectors, we went through several clanging iron doors and entered a large room with small, school-like desks and colored chairs. Two to three guards were in the room at all times, sitting at an elevated desk where they could constantly survey the activities in the room. I looked around at prisoners visiting with their wives or friends in hushed tones so as not to be overheard.

I watched as one very large, muscular man was escorted into the room by an armed guard. The prisoner swaggered into the room with an air of defiance and even showed a lot of attitude toward the young woman who was there to visit him—either his wife or girlfriend. He reminded me of a little kid who was trying to show off in front of his friends.

A few minutes later, another prisoner was escorted into the room. This man's demeanor was totally different from the inmate entering before him. He came into the room with a big smile on his face and immediately came over and greeted his two friends with a hug, the two who were involved in prison ministry.

As he was introduced to us, tears came to his eyes as he realized that I was Rachel's dad. He told me how much her story had touched him, and to my amazement he began to quote from her "Code of Ethics."

Son of Sam—Child of God

The next three hours comprised one of the most amazing experiences I have ever had. I had to keep reminding myself that this was the former "Son of Sam," the man who was labeled a monster because of the horrendous deeds he had committed.

I don't have any supernatural x-ray vision that lets me see into the soul of another person and determine his spiritual state. But I can tell you this: during that meeting I had not one ounce of doubt that I was not talking with the murderous Son of Sam, but was sharing Christian fellowship with a child of God.

David Berkowitz radiated the life of love of Jesus Christ. He wept as he shared of his sorrow concerning his past deeds and of the powerful, life-changing experience he had fifteen years earlier when he had yielded his life to the lordship of Jesus Christ.

My heart goes out to the friends and families of David Berkowitz's victims. I know their pain. I know their sorrow. I know the aching feeling of loss that never quite goes away. I thought of them as I sat talking with this gentle teddy bear of a man who has caused them such pain. I also heard and felt the genuine pain that he now feels for them. The six of us wept and prayed together for those families that day.

As I held David Berkowitz's hand in prayer, I was reminded of the fact that these hands had been redeemed! They once were hands of terror and bloodshed, but now they were hands that ministered love and mercy to others. Hands that were lifted in prayer to a Redeemer who could transform a serial killer into a son of hope!

David Berkowitz with Darrell Scott

Can God truly forgive and change a life as wretched and sinful as that of David Berkowitz? Absolutely! After spending ten years in prison, David had an encounter with God that changed his life.

Another inmate had given him a Bible after telling David that Jesus loved him and could forgive him for his horrible past. At first David mocked his new friend, but one day he began to read from the Book of Psalms. He read that a wicked man called out to God for mercy and forgiveness and that God heard his cry and forgave him, healed him, and set him free. David began weeping as he read those words, and he started down a path of repentance and change!

For a number of years David has volunteered to work with those in his prison who are mentally handicapped. He prays with them, he reads to them, and he loves them with God's love. He goes back to his cell at the end of the day, where he spends his time in personal prayer and reading of Scripture. He then painstakingly answers any letters that have come to him that day.

David will be the first to tell you that he deserves to remain in prison the rest of his life for the things he did. In fact, he sent a letter to the governor of New York asking him to convey to the families of his victims that he sees no need to ever meet with a parole board, and that he wants them to know that, for their sake, if for no other reason, he should never be released.

This man who was once called the "Son of Sam" now wants to be remembered as the "Son of Hope."

I left the prison that day with a new perspective of the amazing grace and forgiveness that is available to anyone who will genuinely repent and accept the salvation God has offered us through his Son. David Berkowitz had come to know more freedom during his imprisonment than many people who live outside of prison walls.

Mysteries of Mercy

After our meeting, David wrote me a letter dated March 31, 2002:

> I cannot begin to tell you how blessed I was to have been able to meet you.
>
> Please greet your family for me and [tell them] *Rachel's Tears* and *Chain Reaction* have been both inspirational and helpful to me. I'm a better and stronger Christian today because of your daughter and her testimony.
>
> D.B.

This letter was followed up by two additional postings on David's Web site:

April 1, 2002

On Friday, March 29th, it was definitely a "Good Friday." For I was both blessed and privileged to have a visit with Darrell Scott. The Lord has broken down the walls between me, a murderer and convicted felon, and a man who lost his daughter to gun violence.

    D.B.

April 20, 2002

I have long ago determined in my heart that I would make Rachel's teachings a part of my life by showing mercy, kindness and forgiveness.

    D.B.

I am continually amazed by the mysteries of God's mercy. Why would God send His Son to earth where He would be crucified for our sins? How could the glorious message of God's grace touch sinful souls like mine and David Berkowitz's?

I may never understand these things in this life. But I do believe that someday, David Berkowitz will have the opportunity to share with Rachel Scott how her life made an impact on his.

nine

Growing Through Grief and Pain

As I was writing the final chapters of this book, I received a call from a friend who had heard a particularly moving testimony about the impact of Rachel's life.

As a parent who has lost a child, I can understand the grief of parents Paul and Julie Davenport, who live in Glenville, New York. The Davenports wanted to share the story of their daughter Shawna.

A Daughter's Death

Shawna Elizabeth Davenport, the oldest of three children, was born on May 21, 1985, and died on May 10, 2002, just eleven days from her seventeenth birthday. Shawna was a passenger in a speeding car that was going too fast to negotiate a curve on a winding country road. The car struck a tree, killing both Shawna and the driver.

Shawna was a junior at Scotia-Glenville High School. She was a gifted musician and was the first-chair flutist and an officer in the school band.

She also was actively involved in the "GIVE" program, a volunteer community outreach sponsored by the New York Governor's Office. With GIVE, Shawna called shut-ins just to bring a little happiness into their lives. She helped disadvantaged children with homework and baby-sat so parents could attend school activities.

Her many friends spoke of her as an encourager and a role model with a smile, hug, and kind word for anyone in need. Most importantly, she loved Jesus. She assisted her mother in teaching junior high girls in Sunday school and volunteered at Vacation Bible School at Faith Baptist Church in Rexford, New York, where she and her family are members. Shawna and her brother attended youth group there on Thursday nights.

Paul and Julie got a copy of *Rachel's Tears* after they attended an event in Albany where I spoke about Rachel. Shawna read the book immediately and came to feel a special connection to those killed at Columbine. Like Rachel, Shawna had endured ridicule for her beliefs and was excluded from some social groups because she did not swear. She would often call her parents to take her home from parties or school events where kids were drinking or doing drugs. Her belief in the sanctity of marriage was best expressed in the inscription on the ring she always wore: TRUE LOVE WAITS. She was not perfect in her walk with God, and often expressed, as did Rachel, the difficulty resisting the temptations and pressures facing teens today. But she persevered the best she could.

Paul and Julie didn't realize how many people cared for Shawna until approximately fifteen hundred people came to her wake and more than eight hundred attended her memorial service. This was quite a statement about a sixteen-year-old girl who shunned the spotlight and was most comfortable spending quiet nights with her family, listening to music, playing her flute, and enjoying pizza and wings. At the service and afterwards, Paul and Julie heard stories about the impact Shawna's kind heart and gentle spirit had, and they listened to the many students who said she was their best friend—many of whom they had never met before. There were also stories about her being unashamed to talk to her classmates about Jesus. It became clear in a short time that she touched the lives of so many people.

Since her death, Shawna's parents have begun hearing from people whom she touched in a variety of ways. This reminds me so much of how we heard from hundreds of people after Rachel's death. One person told Paul and Julie that Shawna always had a kind word for the lady serving breakfast at school. And after talking to a kid with green spiked hair after school one day, Shawna told her parents she thought he really was a nice guy—not quite the same as what others at school thought about this "outcast."

Paul and Julie received a letter from a woman who told of sitting beside Shawna at a local hockey game. She said that Shawna made her laugh all night. In the letter she wrote, "She was a girl with a glowing face, a smile that told you of her inner beauty, and friendliness like I'd never seen in my life. She was obviously a blessing to this world while she was here."

Shawna and Rachel were alike in many ways. Rachel would smile at the thought that she had played some role in another young woman's starting a chain reaction of kindness and compassion half a continent away.

Comfort in the Midst of Troubles

The apostle Paul's second letter to the Corinthian Christians is one of his most honest and personal letters. In it, he responds to church members' criticisms of his behavior and spiritual authority by recounting the many instances where he suffered for serving Christ. The anguished letter overflows with words like *beatings, persecution, danger, hunger, distress, flogged, sufferings, sorrow, and tears.*

But such experiences haven't made Paul angry or bitter. Instead, he opens the letter's first chapter with praises to God and an explanation of the important role suffering plays in the lives of believers:

Praise be to the God and Father of our Lord Jesus Christ, the Father of com-passion and the God of all comfort, who comforts us in all our troubles, so that we can comfort those in any trouble with the comfort we ourselves have received from God. For just as the sufferings of Christ flow over into our lives, so also through Christ our comfort overflows. If we are distressed, it is for your comfort and salvation; if we are comforted, it is for your com-fort, which produces in you patient endurance of the same sufferings we suffer. And our hope for you is firm, because we know that just as you share in our sufferings, so also you share in our comfort. (2 Corinthians 1:3-7)

What a powerful passage so full of hope and encouragement and common sense!

Perhaps the most important point Paul makes is that when we have devoted ourselves to God's service, the pain and sorrow that comes into our lives can be used to provide comfort to others who may be experiencing their own pain and sorrow. This has clearly been the case with Rachel, whose death has helped spawn a renewal of interest in Christian commitment and service. And as for me, the grief and sorrow I have experienced over the past three years have provided comfort to many people who have shared with me about some of the horrible sufferings they have endured in their lives.

Suffering comes in many shapes and sizes, but it all hurts, as the following testimonies demonstrate. On the other hand, all these stories show that our pain diminishes somewhat when we share it with someone else who has had his own painful experiences.

One high school student wrote us because she found in Rachel's example an answer to some of her own suffering:

> I was picked on and made fun of all through my elementary and middle school years because of a speech impediment. There were times when I didn't want to go on living. So, when I stood up to accept Rachel's Challenge, I meant it. I'm going to stand up for the kids who get picked on. I am going to treat people with kindness and respect. I truly look at Rachel Scott as my role model.

An eighteen-year-old high school student from the Philadelphia area talked about facing a variety of problems:

> I have had a rough life, not knowing where I was spiritually. I dabbled in everything illegal from drugs to violence. But I found God. I am newly saved, but not quite able to grasp it all. I am going through some hard times right now. My friends have abandoned me for my newly found faith. I found a book called *Rachel's Tears* and after getting no more than five pages in, it brought me to tears. Just know that your daughter is helping me cope through some hard times.

An eighteen-year-old high school graduate from the Augusta, South Carolina, area, sent us this e-mail:

> About 2 pages into *Rachel's Tears*, I was sobbing right there in the middle of the book store. I suffer from severe depression and anxiety and have been suffering from it since I was about 13. After reading this book, I felt like my mind and soul was lifted above all of the pain and I felt energetic and optimistic (something I haven't felt in years). This book has taken me to levels that I didn't even know existed and I want to stay there. Rachel's death was not in vain at all. It has reached me.

One teenager from Cumming, Georgia, was well acquainted with sorrow and despair:

> I was about to commit suicide. I thought I was not worth [anything]. I had always been raised in the church, I prayed, got baptized. It was not till that night at the teen fest that I decided I was worth [something]. That night I bought journals and started writing in them. My teachers noticed a big change in my attitude. Thank you for letting me realize I needed to change.

Parents often write me because they feel confident that the sorrow I have endured will help me understand their sorrow:

> [A few years ago] we were returning home from a play when the driver of an 18-wheeler truck fell asleep and hit us from behind. My daughter was 16 at the time. She received brain injuries and basically she is a quadriplegic with severe short-term memory problems. She was in ICU for 4 weeks, in a coma 4 months, and in the hospital 7 months. The first thing she said to the nurses when she started talking was "God has a plan for my life." When I fret about her doing something, she just tells me, "If anything happens to me, Mom, it will be a promotion."
>
> I'm so sorry for your loss. I will continue to pray for you because I know the void it has left.

Compared to this mother's pain, the struggles of the following thirteen-year-old girl may seem less significant. But to her, they were just as important, and Rachel's example was just as powerful:

I would like to tell you how wonderful your book is. I was only on the first chapter and I was in tears. Rachel had a very special gift. In my school there is the "popular" crowd and then there is me and my friends. The "populars" yell at us for wearing the same type of clothes they wear and make it their job to make us feel like outcasts. *Rachel's Tears* helped me understand that it doesn't matter what they think. What matters is what I think of myself. Rachel made me think of everything I have and most of all she reminded me of how much God loves me. Thank you for helping me find the real me.

Looking at Life or Seeing Through It

Often when I speak, I talk about two radically different approaches to life. Some people are "look-atters." In trying to make their way through life, these people rely almost exclusively on the evidence of their eyes and their other natural senses. I call them "look-atters" because they spend most of their time examining the surface of things without going any deeper. "Look-throughers" have a totally different perspective on life. These people move beyond mere sense sensations, seeking instead to understand the deeper spiritual reality beneath physical appearances.

I will be the first person to admit that I don't always understand God's will or what He is trying to accomplish in a particular situation. Still, I know that He exists, that He loves me, and that He is active in the affairs of our world. We can't always see precisely what He's doing, but that doesn't mean we shouldn't try to keep our mind and heart open to the possibilities of His presence in our midst.

In the days and weeks after Rachel's death at Columbine, I didn't have any idea of what God was doing. I was experiencing so much sadness and grief that I was pretty much operating like a "look-atter." Of course, in the years since then I have become much more of a "look-througher" as I have been able to see the outlines of God's grander purpose in this tragedy.

I was encouraged to receive the following e-mail from a young man in Wisconsin who had experienced plenty of tragedy in life but was still trying to develop the ability to be a "look-througher":

My life had been a series of disasters. My dad left us when I was young and never attempted to make contact with us again. I have attempted suicide a number of times and have battled depression throughout my life. I am 20 years old, but I feel at times that I've lived over 50 years.

I read the book about your daughter and it really changed me, but I heard you speak at a large youth convention recently, and something you said had an even bigger impact on my life. You talked about being a "see-througher" and not a "look-atter." While you were explaining this, I just went numb! I broke down and began to cry. I realized that I have been spending my life as a "look-atter" instead of a "see-througher."

Rachel's life and your message have permanently changed me. It has been over a year now and I have become a "see-througher," looking beyond the visible to the hand of God at work in every situation, no matter how bad it seems. I want you to know that it works. That secret needs to be heard by everyone on this planet!

The Ultimate Loss

Of course, when we experience the death of a loved one, this is the ultimate loss we can live through, and the ultimate test of our faith in God and our ability to look beyond the sorrow that is so present before us. Knowing that, it has been so encouraging to receive so many calls, letters, and e-mails from people who say Rachel's story has helped them experience God's comfort in the midst of the tragedies of their lives. It's just as Paul tells us: "For just as the sufferings of Christ flow over into our lives, so also through Christ our comfort overflows" (2 Co. 1:5).

It can be hard to believe these words when someone you love has died, but over the past three years, I have received many testimonies from people who say Rachel's death and my talking about it has helped them to reclaim God's spiritual resources for coping with grief.

One young woman sent an e-mail encouraging me to contact her if I needed someone to talk to, writing, "I know how hard this has been for you. In the last year three of my close friends have died. Not the same way, but I know how it feels. If you ever need someone to talk to here's my e-mail address." Another person sent this e-mail from Redondo Beach, California: "I, too, am a victim of a violent crime. My older sister was brutally murdered just one week after her 21st birthday. That was 18 years ago and I still think about her every single day. I feel your pain and your passion and I just hope I can somehow help make a difference."

A seventeen-year-old high school student from Bakersfield, California, said this:

I know how it is to lose people or things you love because [a few years ago] I lost my house. It caught fire and everything was gone. [This year] I lost my grandma. It was hard because two years earlier I lost a friend in a car crash. I'm not trying to say I know how you feel because I don't. I just want your family to know that if you need someone to talk to, I will be here.

A father from Grants Pass, Oregon, shared my grief as a parent:

My son died two years ago.

My wife and I want to encourage you in this time of grief. Our experience has been that the first year is spent in shock. Every day is a new experience because it is the first day without your child. Rachel was a beautiful young lady with a good grasp of what is important in this life. That's the memory you must always come back to.

Another grieving parent sent this message from Nashville, Tennessee:

I, too, am a member of the "club." I buried my second son when I was 26 years old. Twenty years ago. I want everyone I know to see the video [*Untold Stories of Columbine* featuring Darrell telling Rachel's story]. I want all the friends of my two boys to see it. When my two grandchildren are older, I want them to see it. I think the torch will never die, not with a father like yourself, being able to speak the way you do.

One mother wrote about two tragic accidents that happened in her small family, recalling: "We, too, have lost loved ones. I lost a little 5-year-old boy [in] a fatal tractor accident. Two years later I lost my husband [in] another tractor accident. Grief for the loss of a child is the most excruciating pain a parent can live through. We can only tell you that we know the hurt and loneliness you are feeling."

A seventeen-year-old student from New York talked about her grief, as well:

I know what it's like to go through such a horrible experience. This past November my 18-year-old brother was driving with his 17-year-old best friend. His friend got scared when a bus in the other lane was too far over the yellow line. The roads were wet so when my brother's friend went to move over, he lost control of the car. It swerved all over the road, flipped twice and hit a telephone pole. My brother's best friend died and my brother had a broken neck and fractured sternum. It's hard to think that he's not here anymore, but we have to remember all the good times. So I do understand what you're going through a little. But even though Rachel isn't here physically, she is still a role model to everyone.

For the following youth worker from Salvisa, Kentucky, Rachel's story provided a glimmer of hope in the midst of numerous tragedies.

I am a youth worker here. We have had several tragedies here. One of our youth who was supposed to be with us on our Fall retreat never showed up and was in a bad place with bad people and was shot in the head by a young man who was totally disabled by drugs. Another instance was when one of our youth group accidentally ran over his little brother in a pickup truck. Two weeks later the young man who [had] run over his little brother was a passenger in a pickup truck and was in an accident that killed him and the driver. The first death was 1000 yards from the right of the family's driveway, the second was 1000 to the left of their driveway. Thank you so much for *Rachel's Tears*. What an awesome young lady.

The following young person from Defiance, Ohio, has seen more tragedy than many people four times her age. Still, in this letter one can see the persistent struggle to come to grips with it all.

I know what you guys are going through. I don't know if this is any worse, but I have lost all my family members but [my] brother and my mom. Everyone else died in car accidents and was shot at another school shooting. But, hey, we can be in this together, right? I really feel for you guys about Rachel. Life is just not fair. The book on Rachel brought me to tears. It is touching my life.

This twelve-year-old has also seen her share of grief, relating these words: "I cannot even imagine the pain you are going through. My friend died in a fire and I was devastated so I can't imagine what it must feel like to lose a daughter. The article about Rachel in *Teen People* magazine made me cry because my friend that passed away was just like her. She was a friend to everyone and was an enemy to no one.

And this sixteen-year-old high school student wrote us merely to share her own burdens of grief so they wouldn't crush the life out of her:

I would like you all to know that you have my support. I was deeply saddened by what teens are capable of. I found out that a friend of mine was killed in a car accident. I was hurt. This year I had been to three funerals alone. Then I found out that my dad's godmother died. I couldn't take going to another funeral. I was scared and very stressed when I went back to work.

I don't want you guys to feel sorry for me. I think you have enough things to go through right now and I definitely don't need to intrude. I just wanted you to know how I felt.

Seasons of Grief

In the days and weeks after Rachel's death at Columbine, I was shocked to hear some of her closest friends tell me that Rachel had shared with them the insight that she felt would not live to be twenty years old. As Rachel sometimes put it, "I won't live to be old enough to get married."

One of her close friends, Sarah Bay, told us that Rachel had told her on several occasions that she wouldn't live long enough to do all the things that Sarah and her others friends would be doing after graduation. Interestingly, Sarah said that Rachel was never morbid or "down" when she would talk that way. Nick Baumgart, another close friend, said he heard Rachel say similar things as well, and he said that she was as matter-of-fact talking about her death as she was when she talked about having an impact on the world. Nick told us in a taped interview, "Rachel knew she was going to die young and she knew she was going to change the planet. And in the end, that's exactly what she did."

Rachel's cousin, Jeff Scott, had a similar experience. Here's what he told us: "One day just out of the blue she said, 'I'm going to die young.' And we looked at her and said, 'Rachel, why would you say that?' She just smiled and said, 'I don't really know—I just think I'm going to die at a young age.'"

We heard similar stories from Lori Johnson (Rachel's youth leader), Rachel's sister Dana, and numerous others.

Today, I still go to visit Rachel's grave. That's where I do my grieving. And over the last three years, my grief has changed somewhat. Now my sorrow doesn't have that same sting it had initially. At first, every time I thought of her, I experienced that deep, deep hurting inside. I kept expecting to see her bound back into the room at any moment, and I cried tears for missing her.

I don't expect Rachel to show up in the room now, but I still miss her and grieve for her absence. And along with tears of sadness there are also tears of joy. These come from knowing that everything she wanted in life has gone far beyond what she could have ever imagined. She wanted to impact the world, and told me many times she would do so. Today, I am amazed at how her life has impacted so many others.

I couldn't have said this three years ago, but today I am grateful for the grief I have experienced. I believe that there are areas of our own soul that are never touched except through brokenness and pain. I can say without any doubt that in recent years there has been a definite breaking in areas of my life that would have never been touched except for the Columbine tragedy. Like Paul, I believe that God has allowed me to pass through grief and distress in order to feel the kinds of comfort I have never felt before.

I have also experienced new levels of patience. I am often in restaurants these days, and I'm reminded sometimes of how Rachel always looked out for the underdogs in life. This perspective gave her great patience with waiters and waitresses. Remembering this, I have tried to be more patient myself. Some waiters and waitresses have received much bigger tips from me because of Rachel.

Calvary Love

Missionary and author Amy Carmichael lived from 1867-1951. A native of Northern Ireland, she was the founder of the Dohnavur Fellowship, a mission society devoted to caring for needy children in South India.

Carmichael's life was full of tragedy and hardship, but she maintained the attitude Paul talked about. She put emphasis on caring more for others than we care for ourselves. She had a term for this attitude. She called it "Calvary love."

If I can easily discuss the shortcomings and the sins of any; if I can speak in a casual way even of a child's misdoings, then I know nothing of Calvary love.

If I am perturbed by the reproach and misunderstanding that may follow action taken for the good of souls for whom I must give account; if I cannot commit the matter and go on in peace and in silence, remembering Gethsemane and the Cross, then I know nothing of Calvary love.

If my attitude be one of fear, not faith, about one who has disappointed me; if I say, "Just what I expected," if a fall occurs, then I know nothing of Calvary love.

If I say, "Yes, I forgive, but I cannot forget," as though the God who twice a day washes all the sands on all the shores of the world could not wash such memories from my mind, then I know nothing of Calvary love.

If by doing some work which the undiscerning consider "not spiritual work" I can best help others, and I inwardly rebel, thinking it is the spiritual for which I crave, when in truth it is the interesting and exciting, then I know nothing of Calvary love.

If I cast up a confessed, repented, and forsaken sin against another, and allow that sin to color my thinking and feed my suspicions, then I know nothing of Calvary love.

If I am afraid to speak the truth, lest I lose affection, or lest the one concerned should say, "You do not understand," or because I fear to lose my reputation for kindness; if I put my own good name before the other's highest good, then I know nothing of Calvary love.

If I fear to hold another to the highest because it is so much easier to avoid doing so, then I know nothing of Calvary love.

If I myself dominate myself, if my thoughts revolve round myself, if I am so occupied with myself I rarely have "a heart at leisure from itself," then I know nothing of Calvary love.

If I cannot in honest happiness take the second place (or the twentieth); if I cannot take the first without making a fuss about my unworthiness, then I know nothing of Calvary love.

If monotony tries me, and I cannot stand drudgery; if stupid people fret me and little ruffles set me on edge; if I make much of the trifles of life, then I know nothing of Calvary love.

If I want to be known as the doer of something that has proved the right thing, or as the one who suggested that it should be done, then I know nothing of Calvary love.

If in the fellowship of service I seek to attach a friend to myself, so that others are caused to feel unwanted; if my friendships do not draw others deeper in, but are ungenerous (to myself, for myself), then I know nothing of Calvary love.

If I slip into the place that can be filled by Christ alone, making myself the first necessity of a soul instead of leading it to fasten upon Him, then I know nothing of Calvary love.

If I refuse to allow one who is dear to me to suffer for the sake of Christ; if I do not see such suffering as the greatest honor that can be offered to any follower of the Crucified, then I know nothing of Calvary love.

If, when an answer I did not expect comes to a prayer which I believed I truly meant, I shrink back from it; if the burden my Lord asks me to bear be not the burden of my heart's choice, and I fret inwardly and do not welcome His will, then I know nothing of Calvary love.

Do we have this kind of love for others? If not, how do we learn it? I believe the only way we learn about Calvary love is by our own visits to Calvary. It is through grief and sorrow that God comforts us. By doing so, he gives us the spiritual depth and maturity we need to comfort others.

Stop Your Weeping

One time when I was speaking in Kentucky, a young girl approached me and said the Lord had given her a Bible passage for me. She handed me her Bible, which was open to Jeremiah 31:15. Her version of the Bible was a paraphrase, and it featured these words: "A loud voice was heard; Rachel weeping for her children and refusing to be comforted, because her children have died. Thus says the Lord, 'Stop your weeping and dry your tears, for your work will be rewarded. I shall return the children from the land of bondage and bring them back to the land of their inheritance.'"

Now, I know that Jeremiah didn't write that passage with my daughter in mind. In fact, that prophecy was fulfilled twice in Scripture. However, that passage of Scripture brought great comfort to my heart. Especially the part that said, "Stop your weeping and dry your tears, for your work will be rewarded." It was as though the Lord was assuring me that Rachel's death would not be in vain. And neither is the pain and suffering you experience pointless. If you let God control your life, He will use these things to provide you with comfort. And with that comfort, you can reach out to others in a healing and helpful way.

Ten

The Face of Evil
and the Face of Goodness

A few weeks after the killings at Columbine, I was invited to Washington, D.C., to speak to members of the U.S. Congress Judiciary Committee. I opened my remarks with these words: "Since the dawn of creation there have been both good and evil in the heart of men and women. We all contain the seeds of kindness or the seeds of violence."

Some people don't believe there is such a thing is evil. They believe that people are basically good, that the universe is inherently harmonious, and that homicidal criminals are merely emotionally damaged or in need of the right mix of psychiatric medication.

At times I wish I could be so optimistic, but I can't. In our world, goodness and evil coexist and commingle. Once this life is over that will no longer be the case, but for now we must all make our way through a world that is a spiritual battleground between opposing forces.

It's been twenty centuries since Jesus walked the earth, casting out demons and forgiving people's sins. Evil has been present throughout the past two millennia, but sometimes I wonder if events like Columbine have given those of us who are living during this twenty-first century a whole new appreciation for the reality of evil in our midst.

"What Would Jesus Do?"

Evil is not a word that we should toss around lightly, and ultimately, God reserves the right to make the final judgment about the contents of men and women's souls. At the same time, if goodness is to prevail over evil, I believe part of our job as Christians is to "test the spirits" (1 John 4:1) and evaluate the many situations we are involved in.

In the case of the Columbine killings, I believe there is plentiful evidence of evil in the actions of Eric Harris and Dylan Klebold, two troubled young men who recycled their own hurts and hatreds for years and years until their souls were so filled with a simmering rage at the world that evil overflowed their souls and flooded the students and others at Columbine High School.

Rachel knew both boys, but I don't think she ever realized they were capable of performing the acts they did. Most students saw Eric and Dylan as quiet, or rebellious, or as part of a large number of high school students who were social outcasts or merely "strange."

Prior to their violent rampage, much of the two boys' hatred and anger was internalized. Like many, they channeled their alienation and despair into visiting venom-spewing Web sites, or playing violent video games like "Doom," or listening to the music of outrageous but popular recording artists like Eminem, Korn, or shock rocker Marilyn Manson to produce fantasies of bloody revenge.

Then on one April morning three years ago, everything they had stored up for so many years came out with deadly impact.

After the killings, parents of their victims heard rumors that Harris and Klebold had made videos about their murderous plans. For months following the tragedy, no one had seen the tapes or reported on their contents.

That all changed after a reporter for *Time* magazine got access to the tapes, and the twenty-page story he wrote about what he saw appeared in the weekly publication right before Christmas 1999. The magazine featured a controversial cover photo taken by a Columbine security camera showing Harris and Klebold in the midst of their shooting spree. The *Time* story explored the damaged psyches of the two killers, including their anger at blacks, Jews, and athletes and their desire for celebrity, a craving that led them to speculate whether filmmaker Steven Spielberg would consider directing the movie about their lives and deaths.

But there was one important aspect of the killers' motives that *Time* completely overlooked. It was an omission that jumped out at me when I got to see the tapes myself, along with some of the other parents. The grisly pre-massacre home videos I saw made it abundantly clear that both boys shared an intense antiChristian hostility.

"What would Jesus do?" asks Klebold at one point in the tapes, making fun of the popular WWJD slogan that appears on more than a million bracelets and T-shirts. Yelling and making faces at the camera, Klebold asks a second question. "What would I do?" he screams, before pointing an imaginary shotgun at the camera, taking aim, and making a shooting motion and corresponding sound: "Boosh!"

In the same tape, made on March 15, Harris is heard saying, "Yeah, I love Jesus. I love Jesus. Shut the _____ up." Harris later chants, "Go Romans . . . Thank God they crucified that a__hole." Then the two troubled teenagers join together in chanting, "Go Romans! Go Romans! Yeah! Whooh!"

All this was troubling enough, but then I heard Klebold, who had reportedly had a crush on Rachel, single her out for particular disdain, calling her a "godly whore" and a "stuck-up little [expletive]."

Seeing these videos for myself, I began to understand the two Columbine killers' grand design, which, according to a Littleton Fire Department report issued in 2000, included a huge arsenal of weapons and bombs: 49 carbon dioxide or "cricket" bombs, 27 pipe bombs, 11 propane-gas bombs using one-and-one-half-gallon tanks, 7 incendiary devices using more than 40 gallons each of flammable liquid, and 2 bombs they carried into the school in duffel bags, each using 20-pound gas tanks. If more of these devices had worked, hundreds of Columbine students and many teachers might have died that day. I guess we should be thankful that their grand design failed. When it did, Harris and Klebold resorted to killing students one by one.

Still, the killers didn't shoot at random. Rather, they used religion as a criterion for selecting some of their victims. This point was discussed in an April 22, 1999, story in *The Washington Post* entitled "In Choosing Victims, Gunmen Showed Their Prejudice." That story included these two stunning paragraphs:

> While investigators here continued today to sift through the aftermath of the rampage for clues to the shooters' motive, relatives and friends of several of the slain students said that they believe some victims were targeted because they represented all that Eric Harris and Dylan Klebold disdained.
>
> There is no evidence that the murderous pair moved through the corridors with a hit list of names. But it was widely known among Columbine students that the tiny subculture to which Harris and Klebold belonged had little tolerance for devout Christians, or for athletes who favored caps, or for the handful of minority students who attended the school.

It is wrong to kill, no matter who the victims are. But when people intentionally turn themselves against God and against those who serve Him, this is clearly a case of evil.

Evil's Effects

Some acts of evil are more harmful than others. If I curse someone, that hurts them and it hurts me, for I am allowing anger to poison my soul. But if I get guns and bombs and unleash my anger on dozens of innocent victims, the effects of this evil spread much further. In the case of Columbine, the deepest impact would be felt by the immediate families and friends of the victims who died and the many who were wounded.

Behind the headlines of Columbine are hundreds of untold stories about people who lost their sons, daughters, brothers, sisters, or in the case of Columbine teacher Dave Sanders, their father or husband. People everywhere are aware of the Columbine tragedy. What they are not aware of is the ongoing pain and suffering that will continue for many years to come. Every disaster, whether big or small, always results in a chain reaction of pain and sorrow that ripples out from the event in a series of concentric circles.

Holidays for victim's families are always tinged with sadness. My heart aches to see Rachel at our family gatherings. Christmas, Easter, Valentine's Day, and the Fourth of July are all additional reminders of the hole in our hearts. On Father's Day I now receive one less hug, one that I would give anything to experience again. Her birthday and the anniversary of her death are the two days on the calendar that are the hardest of all for me to take.

I sometimes grieve into the future, feeling a sense of loss for the many things I will never be able to see her do, such as watching her graduate from college, walking her down the aisle to the man of her dreams, and enjoying my grandchildren—her children that will now never be born. The consequences of the killers' chain reaction are eternal.

This chain reaction goes beyond the families who lost loved ones to the families of those who were injured. Some of the injured will be exposed to painful operations, physical scars, and wheelchairs for decades; their social and occupational lives will be forever altered; some of them may not be able to have children. All of these situations hold repercussions for generations to come.

There were horrible physical injuries inflicted that day at Columbine, but there were also deep and painful mental and emotional injuries as well. The world will never know the detailed stories of ongoing trauma, paranoia, and hurt to the souls of those teachers and young people who witnessed firsthand the killing spree of Eric and Dylan.

My son Craig is one of those emotional victims. Craig had nightmares about the tragedy for over a year following the event. He will probably always have flashbacks for as long as he lives. Craig was in the middle of the worst of the shooting in the library, and is the only one who witnessed the unfolding horror and also lost a sister or brother. Two of his friends were killed beside him and eight other classmates were gunned down within yards of where he crouched under a desk.

Craig lived in a daze for many months. We kept him out of school the following year because of his inability to stay focused on any one project.

Darrell with sons, Craig and Mike

My son was, of course, not the only one mentally and emotionally scarred by what happened on April 20, 1999. A number of families chose to enroll their children in a different school because of the painful memories. Other families actually moved away from Littleton to try and remove the whole scene from their minds. Craig and my other son, Mike, were given the choice to go elsewhere to school, but both elected to remain at Columbine because of friends.

The Columbine case is unique in many ways, but it illustrates an important fact about the impact of evil. Often, evil acts not only impact the people most directly involved, but they also have a ripple effect that spreads outward, touching others with their darkness and gloom.

A Crisis of Values

As we have seen, events like Columbine cause people to search their souls and ask the "why" questions about the causes of such tragedies. In many cases, one of the explanations for why evil happens is an absence of *good* values.

Cecile S. Holmes is a veteran writer who teaches journalism at the University of South Carolina. In 2001, Holmes wrote a story for *Religion News Service* in March 2001 that featured an interview with another writer named Wendy Murray Zoba. Zoba's book, *Day of Reckoning: Columbine and the Search for America's Soul*, examines some of the underlying spiritual implications of Columbine and other school shootings.

Here is a portion of Holmes' article, which was entitled "Teen Shootings Call into Question Values Taught Young People":

The author of a new book says the recent shooting at California's Santana High School may point to significant cultural problems that cannot be understood without considering their religious dimension.

The lasting impact of what happened in California—and the violence more than a year earlier at Columbine High School in Littleton, Colo.—may be that many Americans reconsider the values being imparted to the nation's youth, says journalist Wendy Murray Zoba.

In an interview shortly after the school shooting in California, Zoba said she worries about the enormous questions posed by such violence.

"Our movies glorify people who lock themselves in rooms and go crazy with machine guns," she said. "It's hard to make generalizations, but we are in a cultural environment that makes it easier to justify (violence) in the mind of someone who is already kind of losing it, going over the top."

Zoba, herself the mother of teen-agers, is a senior writer for the evangelical magazine *Christianity Today* and a former overseas reporter for *Time* magazine. She spent months reporting and reflecting on Columbine and traveled to Littleton, Colo., three times, meeting with students, family members and friends of the victims.

"As a reporter, it was gnawing at me: What happened here?" said Zoba. "And no parent, myself included, can bear the thought that, in our well-ordered universe, kids can be shot execution-style by their class-mates while studying *Macbeth* in the school library."

Zoba believes the Columbine shootings have significant religious impli-cations. The rampage by Eric Harris and Dylan Klebold was described by survivors of the incident as "a spiritual battle" in which a palpable sense of evil was present. But Zoba said she wanted to see the discussion taken beyond debate about gun control, media violence and parenting. In the resulting book, her training in theology lends authority to her exploration of such issues as martyrdom, the existence of evil and the meaning of the cross.

During the final hours of her last visit to Littleton, Zoba sat near the graves. "I wondered how there could ever be enough flowers, pinwheels and Jesus poems to compensate for this loss," she writes.

"There will never be enough blame," Zoba writes. "Brian Rohrbough had called the cross 'a dangerous symbol.' I had come to see it is dangerous, not because it was used to memorialize murderers but because it is the only symbol that can bear the burden of doing so."

Columbine took "us to a place none of us wanted to go," as did the shootings in Santee, Calif., Zoba said. "One of the Columbine students I interviewed inspired me, putting it really well, saying, 'What I'm afraid is everyone is going to look upon us as the generation of the shooters. I want everyone to look upon us as the generation of faithful because we're going to get through this.'"

Zoba urges the nation to examine the fragmented soul-searching of its youth, turning to the work of Christian apologist C.S. Lewis to support that contention.

In his book *The Abolition of Man,* Lewis writes that when young people are raised in an environment where "there is no sense of objective value or absolute truth," they grow up "bereft of that sense of the human disposi-tion that shows grace, restraint and moral fortitude," Zoba said.

"It's that aspect of our human personality that enables us to say no to our visceral impulses. Sadly, it seems that in the age we live in today, we are living in an environment where we are raising young people lacking such understanding," she said.

"The question is not whether or not the killers (at Columbine) asked their victims whether they believed in God," she said. "The larger question that confronted us as a nation was not do we believe in God, but is God relevant?"

The Depths of Evil

For some time after April 1999, the words *Columbine* and *tragedy* were linked in the minds of many people. Over time, that all changed. New calamities came and went. Evil worked its way using a variety of means and resulting in a wide range of pain and suffering.

Today, when people think of tragedy, they often think of another event that was more horrible than anything they could have ever imagined before. I am referring, of course, to the event now known simply as "9/11." I have a hard time imagining anything more diabolical or more birthed in the very heart of evil than the terrorist attack carefully devised to kill thousands of people and break the heart of an entire nation.

Perhaps it is not surprising, but as people struggled to come to grips with 9/11 and understand what it meant, many of them drew comparisons with Columbine.

Horror writer Stephen King made this comparison in the pages of the September 23, 2001 issue of *The New York Times Magazine*:

> It wouldn't hurt to remember that the boys who shot up Columbine High School planned to finish their day by hijacking a jetliner and flying it into— yes, that's right—the World Trade Center.
>
> And now that crazos the world over see that it's possible to get 72 hours of uninterrupted air time on a budget, it will almost certainly happen again.

Pope John Paul II was one of many religious leaders from around the world who quickly issued a statement deploring what he called the "unspeakable horror" of the 9/11 attack. In a telegram sent to President George Bush, the pope said: "Shocked by the unspeakable horror of today's inhuman terrorist attacks against innocent people in different parts of the United States, I hurry to express to you and your fellow citizens my profound sorrow and my closeness in prayer for the nation at this dark and tragic moment."

Another statement from the Catholic Church published in the Vatican newspaper described 9/11 as "acts of madness" that were "diabolically homicidal." "Diabolical minds have carried out and are pursuing monstrous crimes that are sinking humanity in an unimaginable climate of war," the paper said.

Richard Rice, a professor of religion at Loma Linda University, wrote a lengthy article for the journal *Spectrum* in which he talked about how difficult it is for human language to express the true depths of evil:

> The failure of words to capture 9/11 reflects the complexity of the day's events. Unlike other catastrophes of vivid memory, this one will never be confined to a single, mentally manageable event. John F. Kennedy's assassination, the explosion of the *Challenger*, the incineration of Branch Davidians, the bombing in Oklahoma City, the shootings at Columbine High School—like 9/11, these are all events of the you-never-forget-where-you-heard-it variety.

Like many people, Rice expressed concern about the potential abuse of words like *evil* and *hatred*. "They've made their way into newspaper headlines and the covers of national newsmagazines," he said, worried that such rhetoric might cause even more acts of evil if people didn't restrain themselves.

> There's a danger in invoking powerful words like these. Applied not just to actions or events, but to people, to religious systems and cultural perspectives, the word *evil* reflects the very sort of thinking that lies behind 9/11. It demonizes "them" and sanctifies us. If we are nothing but the victims of evil, pure and simple, any reaction is justified, and the spiral of suffering continues.

Still, Rice didn't shy away from using such words himself: "Whatever the complexities of cultural conflict and the intricacies of international misunderstanding, there is no defense for killing thousands of defenseless people. If that isn't evil, it's hard to think of something that is."

Rice also explored an issue that many of us were thinking about: the abuse of Islam by terrorists bent on death and destruction: "Nothing demonstrates the twistedness of human thinking more vividly than using religion to justify mass murder. It seems to confirm the chilling observation I heard somewhere: 'History is filled with good people doing good things and bad people doing bad things. But to get good people to do bad things—for that you need religion.'"

Finally, Rice proposed an idea that has been discussed elsewhere in this book: replacing evil with goodness:

> Perhaps we have heard enough about evil, justice, and revenge. From now on we need to hear more about love and forgiveness.
>
> But do words like this make any sense after 9/11? Can we ever use them with confidence? Is goodness really more fundamental, more representative of our humanity, than a thirst for retaliation and revenge? That's a challenging question.
>
> When we look at it closely, however, we see that that is the question of God. To believe in God is to believe that the forces that work for healing will ultimately wear down and wear out the forces of evil. To believe in God is to believe that love is more powerful than hatred, that forgiveness is stronger than revenge. To believe in God is to let these words define who we are and determine what we do.

Edward T. Linenthal, a professor of religion and American culture at the University of Wisconsin at Oshkosh, shared these thoughts in *The Chronicle of Higher Education*: "This event is so painful, and the scale is beyond anything in American history. I'm reminded of a phrase that people use in Oklahoma City . . . they talk about the 'new normal.' There's a sense in my mind that we live now in a kind of alien, foreboding, frightening landscape, and we're searching for the resources with which to deal with it."

Rather than launching our own holy war on the 9/11 perpetrators, Linenthal urged people to be more reflective: "This is a time to be silent and filled with awe in the face of the power of evil and the enormity of mass death, and not to begin to extract redemption from it. To wriggle out of this horror in redemptive ways is false to the power of the event and dishonors the dead."

What Will You Do About Evil?

Comments like these are sad and sobering, but I don't include them here just to make your heart heavy. Rather, I hope that once we all get over our misconception that evil isn't real or that it doesn't really matter, we will better learn how to combat it.

I want to include a portion of one other article entitled "The Greater the Evil, The More It Disarms." This piece, written by Charles Krauthammer and published in the September 16, 2001 issue of *Time*, recalls an earlier tragedy: the horror of the Holocaust.

Krauthammer wonders why the passengers on the two terrorist-held planes that crashed into the World Trade Center didn't just overpower the terrorists. He likewise wonders why some of the Jews of the Holocaust didn't overpower their badly outnumbered Nazi guards.

The answer, says Krauthammer, is that the airplane passengers never imagined that the plane they were riding would become a human bomb, just as the Jews never imagined that they and their children would be herded into gas chambers. "In all of human history, no people had ever done that," he wrote. "The victims could not plumb the depths of their enemy's evil."

Pursuing this idea further, Krauthammer talked about how years and years of airplane terrorist acts had trained the passengers on 9/11 to expect things to turn out as they always had before.

Decades of experience teach us that if you simply do what the hijackers say, they'll eventually get tired and give up. That's the rule.

But when the rules don't apply, when inconceivably cold-blooded evil is in command, the victims are truly helpless. In the face of unfathomable evil, decent people are psychologically disarmed.

Why then did the passengers on the plane that went down near Pittsburgh decide to resist the hijackers and prevent them from completing their mission? Because they knew: their relatives had told them by cell phone that the World Trade Center had already been attacked by hijacked planes. They were armed with final awareness of the nature of the evil they faced.

Events like Columbine and 9/11 have revealed the true nature and dangers of evil to all of us in ways we never imagined before. Now, having seen things laid out in such revealing detail, what are we going to do about it?

Certainly we cannot turn out backs. We must join the eternal battle and dedicate our strength and energy to the struggle for good.

Seeing the Face of Evil

In the wake of the 9/11 attack, newspapers began publishing photos of the nineteen hijackers. All the men pictured were Muslims religiously and Arabs ethnically. For days, many Americans believed that these men represented a new face of evil for our times.

There were certainly drawbacks in this. After the pictures were published, people in a number of American cities attacked mosques. Some misguided souls even attacked Sikhs, most of whom are from India, and who observe an entirely different religion than Islam.

But soon, one other face replaced those of the nineteen hijackers in people's imaginations. That was the face of Osama bin Laden, the Islamic "holy warrior" who allegedly masterminded the 9/11 attack. As his picture was broadcast and printed all over the Western world, many people began to see his image as the face of evil.

As Americans endured long lines at airport security checkpoints and a series of government warnings that another terrorist attack was imminent, people had no trouble conjuring up an image of what evil looked like. The problem was that many of us didn't have an equally powerful image of goodness that we could call to mind. Evil we could point our finger at; but what did goodness look like in our time of need?

I believe that there is one supreme image of goodness there for us to see if we want to.

Seeing the Face of Jesus

Ken Gire is the author of popular Christian books like *Intimate Moments with the Savior*. Gire talks about the ways many people imagine Jesus as someone who is angry at them for their failures or their sins.

In the following article entitled "He Looks at Me with Delight," originally published in the magazine *Discipleship Journal*, Gire eloquently explores the powerful impact our own mental images of Jesus can have in our spiritual lives.

In the pictures I saw of Jesus when I was a child, he appeared mostly stoic and devoid of extremes. I saw in him neither joy nor sorrow, laughter nor tears, elation nor depression. His facial expressions were all somewhere safely in the middle. Similar to the way he was portrayed physically—not quite a Jew yet not quite a gentile either. Somewhere in between.

The picture of him I remember most hung on a wall in our home. His skin was smooth and tan. His hair, silken and brown. His posture, stately. His features, airbrushed to perfection. His head was turned slightly to one side, his eyes looking away, almost as if he had been posed by a photographer who told him not to look at the camera.

As a kid who got into my share of mischief, snitching cookies from the cupboard or sneaking loose change from my mother's purse, I was glad his eyes looked away.

I remember one picture, though, in which His eyes didn't look away. While on vacation in California, our family visited a chapel where a picture of Jesus was the main attraction. We filed reverently into the wooden pews of the small room, and, as the lights dimmed, we watched the arched doors in front of us slowly open, revealing a huge portrait of Christ.

The eyes were remarkable.

Wherever you sat, they looked at you. Not only at you but through you. Or so it seemed to me as a young boy with plenty inside I didn't want Him seeing. And if that wasn't spooky enough, if you stood up to walk around the room, the eyes followed you. I never knew how they did it. I still don't. But I vividly remember those eyes locked on me with their unblinking scrutiny.

I saw different things in the eyes of all those portraits. I saw detachment. I saw disappointment. What I never saw was delight.

I see it now, though, as I peer into the pages of the Scriptures.

As I read, I try not only to hear what the people heard, but to see what they saw. I imagine, for example, looking at Jesus through the eyes of the hemorrhaging woman (Mark 5:25–34). After His eyes had picked her out of the crowd as the one who touched Him, she fell at His feet, trembling.

When He said, "Daughter, your faith has healed you. Go in peace and be freed from your suffering," I'm sure she looked up at Him. And I try to imagine what she saw in His eyes.

Was it a far-off look? An intrusive gaze into the dark closets of her soul?

I don't think so. I think she saw delight. I think she saw His pleasure in her faith, however brief the touch of her hand, however feeble the grasp on His garment.

On a literal level, the Bible's Song of Solomon portrays the romantic love between a bridegroom and his bride. On an allegorical level, it portrays the relationship between Christ and His bride, the church.

As you listen to Solomon's words, look into his eyes. Can you see the delight in them as he looks into the eyes of his beloved?

"O my dove . . . let me see your form, let me hear your voice; for your voice is sweet and your form is lovely" (Song 2:14, NASB).

"You have made my heart beat faster, my sister, my bride; you have made my heart beat faster with a single glance of your eyes" (Song 4:9, NASB).

"How beautiful and how delightful you are, my love" (Song 7:6, NASB).

It seems impossible, something our thoughts can hardly contain, but, if the allegory holds true, that is the way Jesus looks at us.

In that tonal portrait of Christ, we see the truest expression of how He feels about us. We see it in His eyes. And it's not detachment. It's not disapproval. It's delight.

Anthony de Mellow once said, "Behold God beholding you . . . and smiling." Looking at my bride, who has brought so many smiles to my face over the years, has helped me see what I never could in my youth. That this is a true picture of how God looks at us.

Maybe even the truest.

Another Face of Goodness

One of the things that amazes me as I speak to groups is to see how young people and adults in cities all across the country and around the world have adopted Rachel as a kind of poster girl for goodness. People put her picture on posters or on their school books, like the young person who wrote us from Colville, Washington: "I printed a photo of Rachel and placed it carefully in my binder with her 'My Ethics, My Codes of Life' report. Rachel and her life inspires me to become a better person."

In trying to understand why people who have never met Rachel in person would identify with her so strongly, I have concluded three reasons for it. They are sorry that she died at Columbine; they like the things she said about living her life and her faith; and in a day when evil seems to be active everywhere, Rachel represents a picture of goodness and godliness they can hold on to and celebrate.

The same thing happened with Cassie Bernall, who like Rachel was hailed by many young people as a Columbine "martyr." I get uncomfortable sometimes when people try to portray Rachel or Cassie as if they were perfect or sinless. If you read their books you will see that's not the case.

Still, they were both good girls who tried to be faithful to Jesus in both the big things and the small things of life. If their lives hadn't ended that day, people wouldn't have embraced them as ambassadors of goodness. But somehow, God has allowed them to become symbols of what the Christian life looks like.

When I see people carrying Rachel's picture, I feel conflicting emotions. I am sad to see her smiling face looking at me. But at the same time, I am overcome with joy to see her life providing people with inspiration and a concrete image of goodness in a world gone mad.

So many times in life it seems that we all know what evil is and what it looks like. Goodness seems more mysterious and harder to grasp. If Rachel's face, her words, or her example can help you get a better idea of what goodness is and how it is lived out, that's fine with me. And I think it would be fine with her, too.

Our Unfinished Work

The biggest battle of all time between good and evil happened two thousand years ago on a hill called Calvary. And when seen externally, it must have looked like the forces of evil were going to win the day.

Jesus had been trapped, arrested, tortured, questioned, and hung up on a cross to die like a common criminal. His bruised and bloodied body looked weak and pitiful. And Roman soldiers had mocked His claims of heavenly kingship by putting a crown of thorns on His head. The thorns dug into His scalp and face, causing blood to trickle down like red tears.

Hour after hour, Jesus hung there on the cross, getting weaker by the minute. Gradually His breathing grew slower and more labored and His face grew more pale. Then He uttered three final words before bowing His head and giving up His spirit. Those words were these: "It is finished" (John 19:30).

If you've ever seen movies of the Crucifixion, this is the point in the movie where the violins start playing loudly, the screen gets brighter, and the doves start flying. But there were none of these special effects on Calvary that day. All Jesus' remaining faithful disciples could see was that the man they had followed for the past three years was now dead.

In time, the truth of His final words became clear to them. When Jesus uttered those words, "It is finished," He was referring to His life's mission of redemption for the world.

Many things happened in both the natural and spiritual realms when he uttered that statement. The thick, heavy veil in the temple at Jerusalem was torn in two at the very moment He spoke. The sky grew dark, and the earth trembled.

But dramatic things were taking place in the invisible realm as well. The old covenant that God made with Israel was being replaced by a new one. The laws that were written in stone were now being written on hearts. Law was giving way to grace, and for the first time since Adam was created, humankind could walk in total freedom from condemnation and sin.

Interestingly, one of Rachel's final statements was this: "It isn't finished." She was talking to her teacher Mrs. Carruthers, who had asked Rachel about her drawing showing a pair of eyes crying thirteen tears and watering a Columbine plant.

Rachel's simple words wouldn't make the earth tremble or the sky turn dark. They would not be the key to offering redemption to the world. She wasn't a savior; she was just a high school girl finishing up a drawing.

But the parallels are amazing. Within moments, Rachel would be dead. And now the unfinished work she never got to do is being carried on by others.

Her death that day at Columbine wasn't the end of her mission, only the beginning.

"It isn't finished"!

Her seventeen brief years of life weren't the totality of her life, but they were the period she was given to launch the chain reaction of compassion and kindness she believed would change the world.

"It isn't finished"!

Her desire to "reach the unreached" with the message of Jesus' love didn't stop that day in April 1999.

"It isn't finished"!

Her tears of compassion for the people regarded as outcasts, losers, and underdogs haven't ended.

"It isn't finished"!

And now her tears are being transformed into smiles, because *"It isn't finished"!*

Eleven

The Other Columbine Effect

T*ime* magazine devoted its March 19, 2001 cover and many pages of the same issue to something it called "The Columbine Effect."

"Columbine was not the first mass killing at a school, but it was so ornately gory and so profoundly heartbreaking that it became a cultural reference point," said one of the issue's articles.

For many people, this is the only "Columbine effect" they've ever heard of, but in this chapter you will see the other side of the story. Over the past three years, I have seen how an event that began as a tragedy has been transformed into an episode that has brought many people happiness, joy, and a greater sense of purpose. Good has come from something so bad.

The word *Columbine* is a powerful symbol that means so many different things to so many different people. First, let's take a look at how journalists and other cultural observers have defined the "Columbine effect." After that, we'll look at what I call the other Columbine effect.

Anxiety in the Hallways

Schools are relatively safe places, but that's not the impression some people have.

The journal *Criminal Justice Ethics* reports that more than 99.99 percent of public schools have never had a homicide of any kind, let alone a mass killing. In the 1992-93 school year, there were 54 violent deaths on school campuses. In 2000, there were 16. As Thomas Connelly, a safety consultant who has worked in schools in twenty-two states, told *Time* magazine, "The data suggest that most schools are very safe places for kids, and they're getting safer."

But that's not the way many young people see their own schools. According to *Jane's School Handbook*, a resource used by many schools and districts:

In schools that have experienced gun violence, many children and adults are afraid to return. School officials routinely report decreased attendance of up to 25-30 percent of the student population in the weeks following a violent incident.

In the aftermath of a school shooting—even one hundreds of miles away or in a different country—a sense of fear and distrust of fellow students and the environment can prevent students from re-engaging in the life of the school and the learning process. This traumatisation can lead to physical, cognitive and emotional changes in both children and adults and must be understood, recognised and addressed.

Teachers and administrators already have enough to do, so it's unfortunate that many of them now have the additional challenge of calming anxious students. But this is one sad part of the Columbine effect.

Cops and Copycats

One of the most disappointing results of Columbine is that between sixty and one hundred young people have claimed that the tragedy inspired them to plan and execute their own school rampages. One young man in Port Huron, Michigan, said he wanted "to outdo Columbine," and a high school student in Millbrae, California, bragged to friends that he was going to "do a Columbine."

Sadly, some of these troubled teens saw the Columbine killers as some kind of twisted role models. One young man from Cleveland, Ohio, said he planned to follow their example and "bask in the glory."

There's a reason many of these attacks never happened. That's because students began to take such threats seriously, they reported them to the proper authorities, and authorities took them seriously, too.

"There is this concern that some people have about snitching," said one expert. "But the fact is that moving from the time you hear the remark to a later time, if something drastic happens, you probably for the rest of your life will wish that you said something."

Another expert shared these thoughts with *Time* magazine: "The best metal detector is the student. Snitches are becoming angels." In the wake of Columbine students and authorities are more alert to the possibility of potential threats.

In addition, after the tragedy police have entirely changed the way they respond to problems. "The post-Columbine world is a scary place, and law enforcement officials have to be prepared for it," wrote *Denver Post* reporters John Ingold and Marilyn Robinson. One expert told the two writers that since Columbine, "training for law enforcement officers has undergone a 'fundamental quantum shift.' Officers responding to Columbine sought to set up a perimeter and contain the shooters. Officers in the new world move quickly to chase, find and, if necessary, kill the killers."

One additional post-Columbine change is that many schools have instituted "zero-tolerance" policies that are much tougher on students who violate school policies. "You don't have to bring a gun to school to get suspended. In the post-Columbine era," said a *Time* magazine reporter, "a fingernail clipper will do, or a pair of scissors, according to a Harvard report released last year on zero-tolerance policies against 'weapons.' Of course, nothing could be the same after Columbine."

Stopping the Bullies

Schools have also enacted tougher rules about controlling the bullies in their hallways. Colorado enacted statewide anti-bullying policies in May 2001, following the lead of legislatures in Georgia and New Hampshire.

According to the *Denver Post*, bullies are the cause of numerous problems at schools. "Threats and overt violence also keep more than 500,000 students in the U.S. and more than 10,000 students in Colorado in grades 9 through 12 from going to school at least one day a month, according to the Center for the Study and Prevention of Violence" in Boulder, Colorado.

A number of private individuals and groups have also worked to stop bullying. Peter Yarrow is a member of the folk trio Peter, Paul, and Mary (ask your parents). Yarrow sings a song called "Don't Laugh at Me." The song's chorus features these words:

> Don't laugh at me
> Don't call me names
> Don't get your pleasure from my pain
> In God's eyes we're all the same
> Some day we'll all have perfect wings.

Yarrow's song is part of his partnership with the Kindness Campaign, an effort launched by professor Barry Weinhold at University of Colorado in Colorado Springs. The anti-bullying campaign uses music, video, and classroom exercises to try to eliminate bullying and disrespect. It also invites educators to presentations where they can sign up for a class entitled "Creating Kind and Safe Schools."

Questions About Contemporary Youth Culture

Columbine has also inspired much handwringing and introspection by parents who asked themselves how killers like those in Colorado could scheme and prepare for such an attack without their parents knowing. The reality, as many parents know, is that children often live lives of isolation from parents and all other adults.

Two Christian leaders were among those addressing such concerns. Charles Colson, founder of Prison Fellowship Ministries, wrote these words after the Santee shooting in southern California: "If you're wondering 'Where were the adults?' it's clear you don't know how most American teenagers are growing up today. American teenagers operate in what has been called a 'parallel culture' that operates free of adult interference."

And John Whitehead, founder and president of The Rutherford Institute, a Christian legal organization, added these thoughts:

> Our young people are part of a lost generation—raised in a world where life has little to no value, the almighty dollar takes precedence. Values are taught by prime time sitcoms and Saturday morning cartoons. They are being raised by television and the Internet, and nourished by fast food.
>
> They are seeking comfort wherever they can find it—in sex, drugs, music, each other. They are searching for hope and finding few answers to their questions about the meaning of life.

Although such comments may seem harsh or overly pessimistic, sentiments like these have served as a wake-up call for many parents who are now trying to spend more time with their children, talking to them about their lives and helping them develop positive values.

Kids Respond to the Crisis

These are only some of the effects of Columbine that have been debated by thinkers, writers, and others in our country. But behind the scenes, others have told us what the tragedy and our response to it has done to them.

A woman from Florida sent this e-mail:

My husband and I watched you being interviewed on Fox News tonight. We want to commend you for the powerful message you are sharing around our nation. We had read your speech before Congress and agree wholeheartedly that the issues go deeper than gun control and passing more laws. Your daughter's life is honored by the course you have chosen.

A California father had similar sentiments:

I saw you on *Hannity & Colmes* tonight and I had to send you a message. Your assessment of the root cause to school violence, and perhaps to most violence in our society, is the most intelligent and honest I've heard. I thank God that you have the strength in the midst of your agony, to carry her story to the world—and change lives along the way. Your little girl's story is changing millions of hearts, and I know she's smiling at you.

A teenager from Pennsylvania sent this interesting e-mail concerning Rachel's "electronic" impact:

I just visited the Columbine [R]edemption web site looking for information on Rachel Scott for a religion project. When I typed up her name on the computer 36,000 web sites came up. I couldn't believe that a 17-year old girl had such an effect on the world. That made me look at my own life and examine it and ask questions like how much longer do I really have[?] Your daughter Rachel really does have an effect on me.

Another Pennsylvania teen had this to say:

Rachel is a hero to me. The impact of [what happened] has already affected thousands and will continue to spread. When I think of her, there's a quote [I remember], "How long after you are gone will ripples remain as evidence that you were cast into the pool of life?" Rachel has a lot of ripples because she wasn't afraid to live for God, and I have a feeling that those ripples will continue to spread and send out new ripples.

We even get e-mails from as far away as Europe, one of them asking for Rachel's story to be spread even further: "I'm from Switzerland and now I would like to start a musical with a story about Rachel and Cassie. I believe with this story many of the young people would come to Jesus. I [would] like to ask your permission."

And a Wisconsin student just wrote to let us know she cared: "I just wanted to say that even though I am thousands of miles away, you are in my thoughts often. Keep smiling."

Finally, a Texas man hoped that Rachel's example would inspire the young people he worked with:

> I spent several years as a Youth Minister and enjoyed working with teens that showed commitment like Rachel but I am not sure they would have stood up as Rachel did. In fact, I would like to say I would, but when it all came down I could only hope I would. The message that was told last night touched many lives and the coastal bend area of Texas will never be the same. Thank you for taking such a horrible tragedy and letting God use you to proclaim His almighty power.

We Are God's Hands

Mother Teresa of India was one of the most famous Christians of the twentieth century. She worked with the homeless and destitute people of Calcutta, and continually told people who sought her insight and inspiration one simple message: We are God's hands.

She would explain that God loves people and doesn't want them to suffer. Still, for reasons we can't understand, many people in this world experience horrible suffering in life. Mother Teresa's explanation for this was that we were not doing what we could to ease suffering. God wants to do this, but we are His hands. And if we don't do it, it probably won't get done.

I was thinking about this message last Christmas.

Christmas celebrations have been difficult in the years since Rachel's death. The holidays have been hard for all of us in her immediate family. Before Columbine, I had enjoyed the anticipation of family gatherings where we would eat, laugh, play games, and eventually sing Christmas carols about our Savior's birth before opening presents. But now there was a big, gaping hole in our festivities. Rachel was not there to brighten up the room.

Christmas 1999 was a particularly painful experience. I found myself aching so badly to see her that my only relief would come from visits to her grave, where I could openly grieve. That Christmas Day was a grim foretaste of holidays to come. The next Christmas was a little easier, but it still seemed to me that the joy of celebration would forever be tainted by her absence.

The Christmas of 2001, the third after Rachel's death, was to provide a most amazing, unexpected surprise! I will never forget the moment when I walked down the stairs from my office into the living room of our house near Denver and was jolted from my thoughts by the ringing

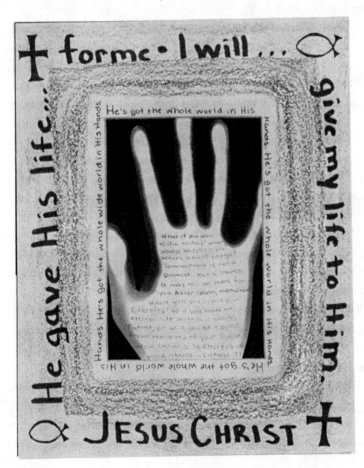

of my cell phone. It was my daughter Dana, who was spending Christmas with her aunt and uncle in Ohio. The first words that Dana practically shouted into the phone were, "Dad, you're not going to believe what we found!"

From the time Rachel discovered crayons, she began to write on anything available! She, unfortunately, discovered paper long after she discovered crayons! We do have scribblings on paper, but only she could interpret some of them. The real problem was that Rachel was not at all confined by paper; she wrote on everything! Walls, floors, chairs, tables, dressers, end tables, and clothing were all fair game for her creative writing and drawing. We have old pieces of furniture and cardboard that will remain in our family indefinitely because Rachel chose to write on them.

One of the creative pieces she wrote was done at school a short time before she died. Rachel drew an outline of one of her hands and colored around it with the colors of the rainbow. She wrote around the perimeter of her hand, but she also wrote a challenge on the inside of her hand imprint. The challenge was to give God a chance with your life. We found this drawing shortly after her death and published it as a poster that now hangs in thousands of young people's bedrooms across America.

We didn't know that two years later we would discover another drawing of her hands that would be even more amazing than the first. But on Christmas Day, 2001, Dana was calling to tell me about another of Rachel's newly discovered works of art.

My mother had given us an antique dresser many years ago. There was a mirror mounted on each end, and when Rachel was thirteen years old, she and Dana wrote all over the back of those mirrors. Dana can recall that day vividly.

The dresser was eventually given to Rachel's aunt and uncle in Ohio. They had it in a bedroom of their home, up against a wall, for a long time. That was where Dana was spending Christmas, and she found Rachel's drawing while there.

A few days before Christmas the dresser had been pulled away from the wall to be moved to a new location. When Dana arrived, she was thrilled to see the things she and Rachel had written years before. Rachel had affirmed her desires to be an actress and a missionary on that day by writing both on the back of one of the mirrors. At the top of the cardboard backing she had written "Someday."

However, the thing that Dana had called me about was an outline Rachel had drawn of her hands. In the center of one hand she had written these amazing, prophetic words: "These hands belong to Rachel Joy Scott and will someday touch millions of people's hearts!"

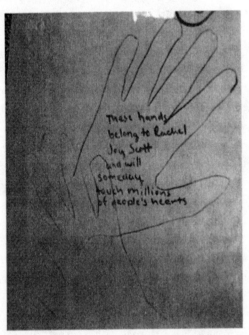

Our whole family was stunned, to say the least. It was as though the Lord had allowed that drawing to be hidden until her prophetic writing could become a reality. By the time we saw this writing, her hands had already touched the hearts of millions of people!

Other Hands of Service

It was years ago that Rachel expressed herself on the back side of this dresser. Her hands have now touched the hearts of many people who, in turn, are using their lives to touch the hearts of others.

Shane Hamman may be the strongest man in the world. He has broken twenty-three American records and four world records. A member of the U.S. Olympic team, Shane appears in the *Guinness Book of World Records* as having squatted with 1,008 pounds on his back! No other man in world history has accomplished that feat! His accomplishments have received widespread media attention. When he appeared on the *Tonight Show* with Jay Leno, Jay asked how much weight he could lift. Shane responded by grabbing Jay and pumping the comedian up over his head!

I met Shane at an Oklahoma youth convention held in 2000, where several thousand young people attended. Shane was deeply moved by Rachel's story. He read *Rachel's Tears* and decided that he wanted to play a part in helping spread her message to teenagers around our nation.

Shane now travels with me occasionally and is in training to speak at high school assemblies with the Rachel's Challenge high school program. He told me that although he has tremendous physical strength in his hands, Rachel had an even more powerful grip in the spiritual realm! Now her hands have touched the heart of the world's strongest man.

Another young man who is using his hands in the service of Rachel's message is Danny Orr, who was a pitcher for the Oakland A's organization until a shoulder injury ended his career. Danny surrendered his life to Jesus Christ as his Lord and Savior at a baseball chapel service. He then became a director with Fellowship of Christian Athletes in his home state of Wyoming.

Danny was there when I spoke to FCA groups in Jackson Hole and Rock Springs in 2000 and was so moved by Rachel's story that he told me he wanted to someday be involved with our organization, Columbine Redemption. That became a reality in the spring of 2002. He has become one of my closest friends and now travels with me regularly as I go out to speak.

Danny, his wife, Jodi, and their three children now live in Phoenix, where he helps coordinate some of our crusade events. In March of 2002 Danny and Don Gordon, the chaplain for the Arizona Diamondbacks (who were the world champions at the time), invited me to attend spring training in Phoenix and speak to a roomful of players and their wives. It was a thrill to meet these pro players from several different teams. A small number of them committed their lives to the Lord that night after hearing Rachel's story, and most of those who were believers rededicated themselves to a deeper walk with the Lord.

Darrell talking with some major league baseball players

Once again, Rachel's hands have touched others. Now today, others inspired by her example are touching people, too.

And the Letters Keep Coming

The Columbine tragedy has upset many people, but for those whose stories follow, the tragedy has served as a challenge.

One university student from Fairfax, Virginia, wrote to tell us that Rachel had inspired her to consider God's calling on her life. "I want to bring joy to people's lives, like Rachel did, and is still doing through her legacy. I have been accepted to go on a missions trip with Campus Crusade for Christ to South Africa and it would be an honor to go 'for' her."

Interestingly, another young woman sensed a similar type of inspiration. I hope these two young Christians get to meet each other!

Rachel had a huge impact on my life. I was just a weak Christian who didn't give a lot of thought to my faith, until I heard her story. I was totally stunned that somebody my age could have that kind of experience with God. When I heard that Rachel had wanted to go to South Africa to do missions work, I made up my mind that I would go in her place, and in her memory, and I did! I am now as serious about my relationship with Jesus as Rachel was—thanks to her!

Rachel's story has also inspired a number of musicians to include her testimony in their music:

Shortly after that event [hearing Darrell speak in Twin Falls, Idaho], I formed a band of young people in my church. We named the band "Rachel's Tears." It was before the book came out. I had no idea at the time there would be a book released under the same title. Within the last six months this group has led many, many people to Christ at our performances. Every time we perform, just before we sing the tribute song to Rachel, I tell the story of Rachel's strength at the time of trial and encourage young people to make a difference.

We also go into youth detention centers and play.

I attend a church in Ontario, Canada, and a friend and I have started a Christian band. I am so moved by Rachel's story and the drawing she did of her hand where she wrote, "He gave His life for me, I will give my life to Him." I would like to use some of her words in that drawing for a song in which we can challenge young people to be sold out to God.

I watched you speak on a video in our youth group tonight. You had me laughing and crying with stories about your beautiful daughter, Rachel. I was glued to my seat the whole night, and when I saw the picture she drew with the fish and the cross, I knew that that was the symbol to be used in our Christian band. I want everyone to hear the story of what her life was about and what she stood for. She is my hero. Thank you for sharing her life with us.

And finally, Rachel's example has inspired one Christian worker to continue her service:

> For the past 2 years I have been living in China. I am now home in Australia, but my calling is to work with orphans in China. I have been struggling with whether I should just stay here in my comfort zone or go back to China. I just came across your book, *Rachel's Tears*, and began reading it. Mr. Scott, I can't even begin to put into words how changed and renewed I am after reading this book! I have recaptured the excitement of God's original calling on my life at age 17 (the same age Rachel was killed). I am now 21, and I know God has used Rachel's life to take me back to the orphans that He has called me to help. Thank you for Rachel and thank you for being obedient to share her life with us.

Columbine has been a significant event in our national history. Its implications have had a ripple effect throughout our culture. But when people talk about "the Columbine effect," let's make sure they are aware of this other side of the story.

$\Big\{$ **Part 3** $\Big\}$

Twelve

A Cloud of Witnesses

When I am in Denver, I make a regular practice of visiting Rachel's grave. Often I will take some flowers with me, and occasionally someone else who has visited her grave before me has already left flowers there as a memorial.

But most of the time I just go and talk to Rachel. I tell her what I have been doing. I describe some of the events where I have spoken, or tell her about things Craig and Bethanee are doing. I tell her about some of the many people we have met, the stories they have told us, and the inspiration they have drawn from Rachel's life and legacy.

I don't know if she hears me, but I do know she is in heaven watching me, rooting me on, and smiling. I know this because one of the most moving passages in the Bible tells me that those who were faithful followers of Christ now look upon those of us who still toil here on earth. Saints from the past are rooting you on, too, even if you never thought about it before. The following Bible passage explains how.

The Essence of Faith

Bible scholars aren't sure who wrote the Book of Hebrews, which—unlike other New Testament books—doesn't identify its author. And they can't agree on precisely who it was written to, or what the exact situation was the author hoped to address. But one thing students of the Bible agree on is that this book contains one of the most beautiful and most powerful descriptions of faith and hope ever written.

It is a lengthy passage which recounts the stories of some of the key figures of the faith, but it is well worth reading and rereading, so I will include it here.

Now faith is being sure of what we hope for and certain of what we do not see. This is what the ancients were commended for.

By faith we understand that the universe was formed at God's command, so that what is seen was not made out of what was visible.

By faith Abel offered God a better sacrifice than Cain did. By faith he was commended as a righteous man, when God spoke well of his offerings. And by faith he still speaks, even though he is dead.

By faith Enoch was taken from this life, so that he did not experience death; he could not be found, because God had taken him away. For before he was taken, he was commended as one who pleased God. And without faith it is impossible to please God, because anyone who comes to him must believe that he exists and that he rewards those who earnestly seek him.

By faith Noah, when warned about things not yet seen, in holy fear built an ark to save his family. By his faith he condemned the world and became heir of the righteousness that comes by faith.

By faith Abraham, when called to go to a place he would later receive as his inheritance, obeyed and went, even though he did not know where he was going. By faith he made his home in the promised land like a stranger in a foreign country; he lived in tents, as did Isaac and Jacob, who were heirs with him of the same promise. For he was looking forward to the city with foundations, whose architect and builder is God.

By faith Abraham, even though he was past age—and Sarah herself was barren—was enabled to become a father because he considered him faithful who had made the promise. And so from this one man, and he as good as dead, came descendants as numerous as the stars in the sky and as countless as the sand on the seashore.

All these people were still living by faith when they died. They did not receive the things promised; they only saw them and welcomed them from a distance. And they admitted that they were aliens and strangers on earth.

People who say such things show that they are looking for a country of their own. If they had been thinking of the country they had left, they would have had opportunity to return. Instead, they were longing for a better country—a heavenly one. Therefore God is not ashamed to be called their God, for he has prepared a city for them.

By faith Abraham, when God tested him, offered Isaac as a sacrifice. He who had received the promises was about to sacrifice his one and only son, even though God had said to him, "It is through Isaac that your offspring will be reckoned." Abraham reasoned that God could raise the dead, and figuratively speaking, he did receive Isaac back from death.

By faith Isaac blessed Jacob and Esau in regard to their future.

By faith Jacob, when he was dying, blessed each of Joseph's sons, and worshipped as he leaned on the top of his staff.

By faith Joseph, when his end was near, spoke about the exodus of the Israelites from Egypt and gave instructions about his bones.

By faith Moses' parents hid him for three months after he was born, because they saw he was no ordinary child, and they were not afraid of the king's edict.

By faith Moses, when he had grown up, refused to be known as the son of Pharaoh's daughter. He chose to be mistreated along with the people of God rather than to enjoy the pleasures of sin for a short time. He regarded disgrace for the sake of Christ as of greater value than the treasures of Egypt, because he was looking ahead to his reward. By faith he left Egypt, not fearing the king's anger; he persevered because he saw him who is invisible. By faith he kept the Passover and the sprinkling of blood, so that the destroyer of the firstborn would not touch the firstborn of Israel.

By faith the people passed through the Red Sea as on dry land; but when the Egyptians tried to do so, they were drowned.

By faith the walls of Jericho fell, after the people had marched around them for seven days.

By faith the prostitute Rahab, because she welcomed the spies, was not killed with those who were disobedient.

And what more shall I say? I do not have time to tell about Gideon, Barak, Samson, Jephthah, David, Samuel and the prophets, who through faith conquered kingdoms, administered justice, and gained what was promised; who shut the mouths of lions, quenched the fury of the flames, and escaped the edge of the sword; whose weakness was turned to strength; and who became powerful in battle and routed foreign armies. Women received back their dead, raised to life again. Others were tortured and refused to be released, so that they might gain a better resurrection. Some faced jeers and flogging, while still others were chained and put in prison. They were stoned; they were sawed in two; they were put to death by the sword. They went about in sheepskins and goatskins, destitute, persecuted and mistreated—the world was not worthy of them. They wandered in deserts and mountains, and in caves and holes in the ground.

These were all commended for their faith, yet none of them received what had been promised. God had planned something better for us so that only together with us would they be made perfect. (Hebrews 11 NKJV)

Wishing or Hoping?

William Barclay was a Scottish Bible teacher whose commentaries on the Bible are both insightful and beautifully written. I think it is interesting to note what Barclay says about the preceding passage:

> To the writer to the Hebrews faith is a hope that is absolutely certain that what it believes is true, and that what it expects will come. It is not the hope which looks forward with wishful longing; it is the hope that looks forward with utter certainty. It is not the hope which takes refuge in a perhaps; it is the hope which is founded on a conviction … The Christian hope is more than hope; it is hope that has turned to certainty.

I don't know about you, but there are times in my life where hope feels anything but certain. Like everyone, some of my hopes have been disappointed and dashed.

On April 20, 1999, I hoped that Rachel would survive the shootings at Columbine as Craig had, and that I would see her beautiful face once again. As the day dragged on and I saw hundreds of students who had survived being hugged by their parents and taken back to the safety of their homes, that hope grew weary. When I was notified that Rachel had been killed, that hope was extinguished.

But the thing we need to remember is that our hope in God is based on something more substantial than any other hope we have in life. It is this deeper, more abiding faith in God and hope in His ultimate purposes that the writer of Hebrews hopes to inspire us to grasp.

Our Heavenly Onlookers

Having written about faith and hope as seen in the lives of deceased saints from ages past, the author of Hebrews next tries to encourage those who are still alive to cling to their faith for all they are worth:

> Therefore, since we are surrounded by such a great cloud of witnesses, let us throw off everything that hinders and the sin that so easily entangles, and let us run with perseverance the race marked out for us. Let us fix our eyes on Jesus, the author and perfecter of our faith, who for the joy set before him endured the cross, scorning its shame, and sat down at the right hand of the throne of God. Consider him who endured such opposition from sinful men, so that you will not grow weary and lose heart.
>
> In your struggle against sin, you have not yet resisted to the point of shedding your blood. (Hebrews 12: 1-4)

Again, I turn to William Barclay, who writes: "This is one of the great, moving passages of the New Testament, and in it the writer to the Hebrews has given us a well-nigh perfect summary of the Christian life."

Barclay also explains this passage's reference to the "great cloud of witnesses." These four words provide the basis for my certainty that Rachel and other deceased Christians now look on as we who live try to follow Christ in our daily lives.

"They are witnesses in a double sense," writes Barclay, "for they are those who have witnessed their confession to Christ and they are now those who are witnesses to our performance. The Christian is like a runner in some crowded stadium. As he presses on, the crowd looks down;

and the crowd who look down upon him are those who have already won the crown."

I don't understand the details about how all this works, and I probably won't understand it fully until I myself become a member of the great cloud of witnesses. I am reminded of the words of Paul in 1 Corinthians 13, the famous "love" chapter. Toward the end of that chapter, in verse 12, Paul writes this moving message: "Now we see but a poor reflection as in a mirror; then we shall see face to face. Now I know in part; than I shall know fully, even as I am fully known." This pretty much sums up the way I feel about many of the mysteries of the faith. There is so much I don't know. But my ignorance doesn't change the fact that God has told me this is the way it is.

As I said at the beginning of this chapter, I don't know if Rachel hears me when I go to her grave and talk to her, but I know she and others watch from heaven, observing everything each one of us does. I know it because God's Word tells me it is so.

My prayer is that these pioneers of the faith will find my work on earth worthy of their praise. I pray the same for you.

Another Time, Another Crowd

I was thinking about this idea of the cloud of witnesses on May 18, 2002. That was the day thousands of students, friends, and parents attended the graduation ceremony of Columbine's class of 2002.

Parents and other loved ones typically regard a graduation ceremony as one of life's special times of transition, but there was nothing typical about this event. Most of the 457 seniors who graduated that day were freshmen when death and destruction turned an average school day into a hell on earth. And many of the symbols of the ceremony paid tribute to that connection.

The class song was "Bittersweet Symphony," a British rock band's melancholy hit. The class motto read: "We enjoy warmth because we have been in the cold. We appreciate light because we have been in the darkness. We can experience joy because we have known sorrow."

And as each student walked across the stage in the outdoor amphitheater at Fiddler's Green, each wore a hat adorned with one tassel. That's the normal procedure for such events. But when the students received their cherished diplomas, they were given a second tassel in memory of their fellow classmates who had died.

Graduating senior Jamie Conwell pretty much summed up the mood, telling Lynn Bartels, a reporter with the *Rocky Mountain News*: "Our class doesn't know normal. We've never had normal. When people say we're going back to normal, it's not possible. After April 20th, we don't know what normal is."

Bartels also interviewed my son Craig, who was a sophomore when the tragedy happened but took a year off for healing and counseling before graduating with those who had been freshmen. He had watched as close friends Isaiah Shoels and Matthew Kechter were murdered, as the three huddled under a table in the library killing ground. Craig's comments reflected his deep faith in God that has sustained him these past three years, and his unshakable hope that good will come out of the horrible evils committed at his school.

"A lot of people, when they look at Columbine, see a bloody tragedy," he told the journalist. "I've been able to see through Columbine to an invisible God behind it who is working his hand for the good. I've seen a lot more good come from Columbine than the bad."

The article described how the tragedy had challenged Craig's lukewarm understanding of God and forced him to confront deeper realities. As Bartels wrote: "Craig Scott, the boy who scoffed at his sister's devotion, prayed as he lay with the bodies of Isaiah and Matt. Then he was able to move, to breathe, to think. He said he heard God's voice telling him to get out of there."

There were other journalists watching the graduation ceremony as well, and they also talked to Craig. An Associated Press story featured this revealing comment, in which Craig refers to the class song:

It's bitter that this is the last class because we shared a bond with each other. But it's sweet because we made it through together. We are living proof that tragedy will not prevail. Rachel's legacy has impacted more people's lives than the negative impact of Eric and Dylan.

I've seen so much good happen from Columbine. As you go through something hard and still try to do what's right, you come out on the other side with compassion.

And Bartels reported another of Craig's insightful comments: "Two thousand years ago, there was a teacher and 12 students who impacted the world. Two thousand years later, there was a teacher and 12 students that I believe have really impacted, in a spiritual sense, this generation. I totally know the Columbine shooting was more than just a school shooting, that it was a spiritual event."

There were a number of speakers at the ceremony, and many of them echoed some of the themes Craig had discussed.

Columbine principal Frank DeAngelis, a man of faith who has been a beacon of strength for many of the students and families, said, "You were forced to grow up far too quickly, and you were denied a normal high school life." But he didn't stop there, adding, "I truly believe that you have gained strength because of the obstacles that you have had to overcome."

Another person who rose to the podium that day was even more upbeat. Student commencement speaker Fletcher Woolsey made a bold prediction to the attentive audience: "I know that this group can lead the world into an age of unequaled peace and prosperity."

I was there in the crowd looking on as the names of all the students were called out and as, one by one, they went forward to receive their diplomas. One of the young men, an honor student, hobbled across the stage with the help of crutches. His body bore the physical scars of an event that left others with inner scars.

Then Craig's name was called and he made his way to the stage. He walked across the platform to receive his diploma and his memorial tassel. And as he left the stage, Craig did something unusual. He danced a little jig of joy.

Tears were already flowing from my eyes as I saw Craig get his diploma, but when I saw him dance, the flow turned into a torrent. Through my tears, I mumbled to Craig and to myself and to God: "Dance your heart out, Craig. You deserve it."

Is this the way deceased saints feel when they see us and share our joy?

An Even Larger Audience of Witnesses

Five days later, Craig got to share his story with a nationwide television audience of millions as he appeared on a broadcast of Oprah Winfrey's popular show. The respected host began with an introduction that set the stage for Craig and his mother, Beth Nimmo.

"We were all frozen in shock as television crews reported live from the scene of a murderous rampage at Columbine High School," said Oprah.

I will always, always remember the young student who gave his riveting account on the *Today Show* the day after the horror.

A 15-year-old freshman on the day of the massacre at Columbine High School, Craig Scott witnessed the unimaginable. To save his own life Craig played dead and prayed to God for courage. Craig survived only to be faced with more devastating news. His 17-year-old sister, Rachel, was dead. She was one of the first students shot and killed on that tragic day.

Following this introduction, Winfrey had the following exchange with Craig:

OPRAH: How have you gotten through it?

CRAIG: There were lots of things that helped me get through. The number one thing that helped me get through was my faith in God. And His grace really came over me especially right after Columbine and helped me heal mentally and spiritually.

OPRAH: You took off the first year, right? You couldn't go back to school?

CRAIG: Yes, that was a really helpful and healing year for me to take off. I did do some counseling. Probably the next thing was all the support that I received. I have such a wonderful, loving family. My mom was there with me all the time and helping and also just our community received an outpouring of love and support from all [over] the world.

OPRAH: What was it like going back to school, even after taking a year off? Did all the memories come flooding back?

CRAIG: I wasn't going to let fear hold me back from reentering my school, and I see Columbine differently than most people. Most people see it as a tragedy, and I really do see triumph when I see Columbine. I didn't have any fear. I even know on that day that God was in control. And it was a wonderful two years. The teachers and the students were really supportive of me and we just graduated and it just proved that tragedy wasn't going to win but triumph would prevail.

OPRAH: Were kids nicer to each other though? Do you think people got the lesson of not ostracizing other kids?

CRAIG: Right afterwards there was a real sense of unity and sincerity and tenderness. I think when tragedy hits differences are put aside and people are unified. And we were so close right afterwards and I think it tends to fade, but there are things that I think were permanently gained: character, I've seen character in myself and other students at Columbine and a sense of compassion which is I think one of the things my sister was all about, she was about being compassionate and showing kindness especially to kids at school that felt on the outside or that didn't receive a lot of attention.

Once again, I could imagine Rachel looking on from heaven, smiling.

Rachel Smiles

Hebrews gives us a roll call of heroes of the faith. It speaks of Enoch, who walked with God until God took him; Noah, who obeyed God even though it cost him the ridicule and scorn of friends and neighbors; as well as other men and women like Abraham and Sarah, Isaac, Jacob, Rahab, Moses, and many others who refused to give in to the seductions of this life, but lived a life of devotion and faith.

These people are our "great cloud of witnesses" who encourage us to run the race that is set before us, always fixing our eyes on Jesus—not ourselves or our circumstances!

I believe that Rachel is now a member of this great cloud of witnesses. I don't say this because she is perfect. None of us is perfect but Christ. But I believe she has become one of the many heroes of faith that "fought a good fight, finished her course, and kept the faith." Her death came much more quickly than early believers who experienced excruciating deaths in a Roman coliseum, but like these saints, she died with an affirmation of her faith on her lips as she passed from this earth.

As a part of this "great cloud of witnesses," Rachel would want you to be challenged to surrender your heart, your life, your will, your future, and your work to Jesus.

My wife, Sandy, challenged me to write a poem honoring Rachel that would match the title of this book. That night, I went to bed thinking about it. I woke up the next morning at 3:15 A.M. with the beginning of this poem going through my mind. I quietly got up and went to our guest bedroom and wrote the following words:

> The 13 tears fell from her eyes
> And Jesus heard her heartfelt cries
> Tears turned to blood that brought us pain
> But Rachel's death was not in vain!
>
> She prayed a prayer—"Oh, God use me"
> To reach the lost—To help them see
> That you're alive—The great "I AM"
> I want the world to "Watch the Lamb"!
>
> Her tender voice so young and brave
> Can still be heard beyond the grave
> And millions now have felt the touch
> Of loving hands that gave so much

She dared to dream—my little girl—
That through God's grace she'd change the world
Her heart of faith was like a child's
Now Rachel's tears have turned to smiles!!!

From Tragedy to Triumph

Our first book, *Rachel's Tears*, closes with these words from Rachel: "This tragedy shall be turned into triumph by the grace of God." I would like to end *Rachel Smiles* with a slight change of wording: "This tragedy *has been* turned into triumph by the grace of God!" Clearly, this is the message of the past three years and of so many of the stories you have read in the preceding pages.

As Psalm 126:5 says, "They that sow in tears shall reap in joy" (KJV). For me, this verse sums up the Columbine experience in nine simple words. Rachel's tears have been transformed from tears of sorrow into tears of joy, complete with a big, heavenly smile!

Many times Rachel prayed this prayer: "God, I want you to use me to reach the unreached." Within three years of her death her hands had touched the hearts of millions and her testimony had pointed the way for untold thousands to begin a genuine relationship with their heavenly Father through a life-changing knowledge of Jesus Christ.

Rachel wrote a poem when she was twelve years old that has become one of my favorites. It reads:

> Father, reach out your hand
> Take hold of my life
> Open my eyes to your wonderful light
> Fill me up with your undying love
> And save me a place
> In your Kingdom above

In death that prayer has been fulfilled.

I look forward to the day when I will be able to look at Rachel in person and once again see the smiling face I remember so clearly. As a fifty-three-year-old man, I realize that day is not too far off. But until then, I look to heaven.

When I do that, I see Rachel smiling.

Conclusion

Many people have wanted to know how they can contact us. Others have asked about the location of Columbine High School and Rachel's grave. Here are the answers to those questions:

Our Web Sites

www.columbineredemption.com
www.rachelscott.com
www.christianamerica.com

The Web sites list our address, phone numbers, and how to e-mail us.

Location of Columbine High School

Because of the tremendous amount of publicity, many people have wanted to see the school. Please be sensitive to the fact that thousands of people have driven by there over the last few years. Please don't intrude into the school itself during school hours, and respect the rules in place to protect the students from constant "curiosity seekers."

Columbine High School is located near the southwest corner of Bowles and Pierce streets in Littleton, Colorado. From I-25 you would go west on either 6th Avenue West or Hampden Avenue to Wadsworth. Go south on Wadsworth to Bowles. Go east (left) on Bowles to Pierce and turn south (right). The school is visible about two blocks down on the left hand side (west).

Rachel's Grave

From I-25 go west on Arapahoe Road to Colorado Avenue. Turn right (north), go about two blocks, and you will see the mortuary on the right-hand side. The large cemetery is behind the mortuary, and you can ask for directions to the Columbine Memorial site or you can turn left into the cemetery and drive to the back side, looking for the thirteen crosses that mark the site. Rachel's body is buried by the thirteen crosses. Her spirit is in heaven.

At Rachel's gravesite

If You Want to See Her There Someday, Follow These Directions

Yield your life to your Creator and receive the greatest gift God has to give us: His son, Jesus. Simply accept His forgiveness for all that you have done wrong and ask Him to cleanse you of all your sin, your guilt, your inadequacy, your faults, your failures. Begin to talk with Him on a daily basis and read His instructions for your life, the Bible. Also, find other believers who can help you grow, and spend time with them. God will lead you to the right group of people to fellowship with. He will place people in your life who can help mentor you through teaching, books, tapes, CDs, and otherwise.

Contact us and we will be glad to help you as much as possible in starting down this new path the right way. May this book spark a new life for some and a challenge for the rest of you, to *know God, be strong, and do great things!* If you do those things, you will contribute to Rachel's smile.

Rachel, I love you.

Dad

LaVergne, TN USA
10 December 2010
208203LV00003B/42/P